D1030869

THE NEW NATURALIST
A SURVEY OF BRITISH NATURAL HISTORY

THE MOLE

THE NEW NATURALIST

THE MOLE

KENNETH MELLANBY

*With 18 photographs and
35 text figures*

COLLINS
ST JAMES'S PLACE, LONDON

William Collins Sons & Co Ltd
London · Glasgow · Sydney · Auckland
Toronto · Johannesburg

First published 1971
Reprinted 1974

© Kenneth Mellanby, 1971

ISBN 0 00 213145 5

Made and Printed in Great Britain by
William Collins Sons & Co Ltd Glasgow

CONTENTS

ILLUSTRATIONS

TEXT FIGURES

AUTHOR'S PREFACE

My purpose in writing this monograph is to give a general account of the mole and of the way in which it lives. I have studied moles for some years, both in the field and in the laboratory. I am fortunate in working adjacent to Monks Wood National Nature Reserve, an area of 387 acres of mixed deciduous woodland which, though it has been managed and exploited in various ways throughout the last 1,000 years, has nevertheless been covered with trees over most of its area for the whole of that period. Monks Wood is, in fact, one of the comparatively few remaining areas of the forest which covered most of England before man removed it and developed the land for agriculture. Most of the indigenous animals of Britain lived in this forest, and were adapted to woodland conditions. When the forest was cut, some species were exterminated. Others adapted their lives to the agricultural landscape, and the ecological importance of the hedgerow is that it provides habitats for many formerly exclusively woodland birds, mammals and invertebrates.

Although originally a woodland animal, the mole found no difficulties in adapting its way of life to the conditions produced by man. So much is this the case that many people always think of moles as primarily denizens of grassland, though, at any rate on the heavy soils such as we find in Huntingdonshire, grassland was produced by man and is entirely dependent on his activities (including those of his grazing farm stock). Moles thrive on grassland, but they can also live in arable fields, though here they may need hedges or ditches as refuges when cultivation is in progress. The enormous hedgeless "prairies" of East Anglia have no moles except near their edges.

Most research on moles has previously been done on farmland which, as I have just pointed out, is an unnatural and man-made habitat. For this reason I think that I had an advantage over those who have studied moles exclusively in grassland or in arable fields, in that the animal's behaviour in its original habitat – woodland – may make it easier to understand more of its economy and of its way of life.

In recent years many scientists have made important contributions to our knowledge of the mole. Much of the earlier work is still valuable on account of the record of observations of mole behaviour, but it is often anecdotal and it is sometimes difficult to distinguish fact from fable. However, there is much to be learned from the first-hand experiences of countrymen, and I have been fortunate to know Arthur Randell, author of several books on life in East Anglia, including *Fenland Mole-catcher*. I have learned much from his reminiscences, his observations and his descriptions of trapping methods used by his father and grandfather well over 100 years ago. One important and thorough scientific investigation was that of Dr L. Harrison Matthews on the sexual cycle, a subject previously confused by folklore and mythology. Further progress on this subject has been made by Dr Ruth Deansley. Then in the 1950s Dr Gillian Godfrey (now Mrs Crowcroft) made striking advances by studying the mole using the technique of attaching a radioactive ring around the animal's tail and then recording underground activity by means of a Geiger counter. We are also indebted to Dr Godfrey and her husband for their useful book on *The Life of the Mole,* now unfortunately out of print. The sense organs, their anatomy and their functions, previously a subject of much confusion, have been scientifically and most ingeniously investigated by Dr T. A. Quilliam and several of his colleagues. Dr Quilliam was also responsible, with the support of the Ciba Foundation, for organising a most valuable two-day symposium attended by many of those studying moles in 1966. A fascinating and unique study has been made by Dr J. Haeck, who followed the invasion of the new polders in the Netherlands, taking advantage of the production of large areas of virgin soil to investigate many facets of mole movement and the colonisation of previously-uninhabited territory. Several scientists in the Ministry of Agriculture, Fisheries and Food, in particular Mr A. J. B. Rudge, have also made important advances in knowledge. In addition to these studies in Britain, work on mole behaviour and physiology, and on such subjects as techniques used in age determination, has been done by other European workers, and important publications have been produced by several scientists, including I. Grülich, G. H. W. Stein, S. O. Oppermann and S. Skoczen.

Notwithstanding all this important work on the mole, there is still much to be done. As is shown in this book, we understand very little about the animal's territorial behaviour, and other problems will not be solved until moles can be reared in captivity. There is still much to be seen in the field by amateur observers, and, if we cannot tolerate moles on our farms or in our gardens, a really satisfactory and humane method of control still awaits discovery. I hope this book will do something to stimulate others to continue this work.

ACKNOWLEDGMENTS

In the text I express my indebtedness to several other workers on the mole from whom I have received information and help. In addition I wish to thank Dr J. Sheail for finding many historical references, and Mrs K. B. King for her help with the scientific literature. Dr N. E. Hickin kindly provided the drawing of a Mole (Fig. 1) and Mrs Alison Leadley Brown that of the front leg of a mole cricket. I am grateful to Mrs Gwen Webb for her drawings of mole dissections, and to her and her husband, Professor J. E. Webb, for discussions on the animal. Dr Oliver Impey kindly supplied the Japanese drawing of *Talpa micrura*. Mr A. J. Frost has given most valuable help with field work for several years, and his practical experience has been of much value. Mrs Rita Duffey has typed the text and corrected both my spelling and the proofs with expedition and accuracy. Finally I must thank Mrs Jean Mellanby for the more literary references, for her encouragement in this work, and for putting up with living moles in the house and the garden without complaint.

CHAPTER I

INTRODUCTION

EVERYONE has seen molehills, but comparatively few people have actually handled a dead mole, while even fewer have touched, or even seen, a living mole. Moleskins were commonly worn as coats by fashionable ladies and as waistcoats and caps by rural dandies up till some thirty or forty years ago, but to-day the fur is almost unknown in the trade. The mole-catcher is a dying profession, and even when moles are controlled on a farm or estate, poisons which kill the animals underground are used and the corpses are seldom recovered. Yet interest in moles is widespread, perhaps because, though they themselves are so elusive, their "molesigns" are so obvious and ubiquitous.

Some of this interest probably arises from exposure in early childhood to Kenneth Grahame's delightful book, *The Wind in the Willows*, and to the dramatised version, seen at Christmas on the London stage, *Toad of Toad Hall*. Although in this play Mr Richard Goolden has for many years given a striking performance which exudes the very essence of "moleyness," yet it must be admitted that this arises from his skill and perception as an actor, and that Kenneth Grahame does not really contribute very much to our knowledge of the habits and behaviour of moles. Nevertheless, his writings arouse our real curiosity, even if the affection they encourage may seem to be misplaced when we know a little more about the habits of this animal!

The mole had one glorious incursion into history, when in
1702 King William the Third's horse stumbled over a molehill,
with fatal results to the rider. This gave rise to the famous
Jacobite toast to "The little gentleman in black velvet." It is
also said by some historians that William Rufus may also have
died in 1100 in a similar accident, and not by getting in the
path of a carelessly aimed arrow. I know of no other serious
accidents caused by these burrows and hills, but at an Open
Week at Monks Wood Experimental Station in 1970 visitors to
the refreshment marquee often stumbled until a notice was
displayed saying "The floor is riddled with mole burrows. Do
not fall in." *The Times* newspaper reported this, commenting
that it was a case of "Nature in the raw."

All moles caught in Britain are specimens of the European
Mole, *Talpa europaea* Linnaeus. The word "mole" is derived
from the Middle English form "molle" or "mulle," though
according to some it is a shortened form of the old name
"mouldwarp" or "mowdiwarp," which derives from the Old
English "molde," meaning "earth," and "werpen," meaning
"to throw." This graphic name of "earth-thrower" persists in
German, where the mole is "Maulwurf," and in Danish,
"muldvarp." Another old name for the animal is "wente" or
"wante."

Many authors have mentioned the mole, with greater or
lesser accuracy. Sir Thomas Browne, in the seventeenth century,
though erroneously assuming, as did many others, that moles
lived at least partly on vegetable matter, yet evidently had
some experience of their behaviour. He writes:

"Other concerns there are of Molls . . . as the peculiar formation of their feet, the slender Ossa Fugalia and Dogteeth,

and how hard it is to keep them alive out of the Earth. As also the ferity and voracity of these animals; for though they be contented with Roots and stringy parts of Plants or Wormes underground, yet when they are above it will sometimes tear and eat one another, and in a large glass wherein a Moll a Toad and a viper were inclosed, we have known the Moll to dispatch them and devour a good part of them both."

Many authors quote the writings of the Count de Buffon, though his account which appeared in the eighteenth century is often more imaginative than factual. Thus he speaks of their domestic life in the following somewhat romantic terms, though the actuality (see p. 49 below) is that the only amicable contact between the sexes seems to be at the moment of pairing:

". . . so lively and reciprocal an attachment subsists between the male and female, that they seem to dread and disrelish all other society. They enjoy the placid habits of repose and solitude: the art of securing themselves from disquiet and injury; and of instantaneously forming an asylum, or habitation, of extending its dimensions, and of finding a plentiful subsistence without the necessity of going abroad. These are the manners and dispositions of the Mole; and they are unquestionably preferable to talents more brilliant, and more incompatible with happiness than the most profound obscurity."

In 1828 W. G. Lewis describes, often accurately, the life of the mole. The following passages illustrate his approach.

"This solitary mischievous animal is disseminated over the greatest part of the world, and appears adapted to a life of darkness. Although it is doomed to hunt for its prey under ground, and usually denied the cheering light of the sun: yet no animal appears fatter, nor has a more sleak and glossy skin. Indeed so perfectly is it suited to its way of life, that it probably enjoys no inconsiderable share of felicity, and is exempt from many evils to which other creatures are liable."

"It was formerly the common opinion that the mole is wholly blind; but, by the assistance of the microscope, it has been found that, though its eyes are small and almost concealed, they possess every part requisite for distinct vision."

"but when the worms are in motion, and approaching the surface of the earth, particularly after rain, it pursues them with much animation; and then it throws up the hillocks which prove so detrimental to the farmer. The fecundity of the mole is very great."

There are many references to moles in Churchwardens' accounts, particularly in the sixteenth and seventeenth centuries. The 1566 Act of Parliament "For the Preservation of Grain" deals with all manner of so-called vermin, and includes the mole in this category. We find many accounts of payments for the destruction of moles, and it is surprising to find how highly this service was rewarded. In one case we read "for the Heades of everie Moulewarpe or Wante, one halfpenny." In 1700, the annual fee of the mole-catcher of the parish of Billingham is one pound, and at Arlesey in 1752 ninepence is paid for the destruction of six moles. As is usual with such efforts in pest control, the mole population does not seem to have been greatly affected. Mole numbers only decrease when their habitat is destroyed (as already mentioned, very large arable fields with no refuges during ploughing contain no moles) or when poisoned baits are generously distributed (see p. 137).

The mole is mentioned in several works of fiction and is the subject of many poems. In fiction the most acute observer is D. H. Lawrence, always perceptive in his descriptions of wild animals. In a short story, *Second Best*, he describes how a girl saw a mole come out of the ground and caught it. The passage quoted below does indeed describe the experience of anyone who has similarly caught and held a live mole.

"The two girls sat perfectly still. Frances watched certain objects in her surroundings; they had a peculiar, unfriendly look about them: the weight of greenish elderberries on their purpling stalks; the twinkling of the yellowing crab-apples that clustered high up in the hedge, against the sky: the exhausted, limp leaves of the primroses lying flat in the hedge-bottom: all looked strange to her. Then her eyes caught a movement. A mole was moving silently over the warm, red soil, nosing, shuffling hither and thither, flat, and dark as a shadow, shifting about, and as suddenly brisk, and as silent, like a very ghost of *joie de vivre*. Frances started, from habit was about to call on Anne to kill the little pest. But, to-day her lethargy of unhappiness was too much for her. She watched the little brute paddling, snuffing, touching things to discover them, running in blindness, delighted to ecstasy by the sunlight and the hot, strange things that caressed its belly and its nose. She felt a keen pity for the little creature.

'Eh, our Fran, look there! It's a mole.'

Anne was on her feet, standing watching the dark, unconscious beast. Frances frowned with anxiety.

'It doesn't run off, does it?' said the young girl softly. Then she stealthily approached the creature. The mole paddled fumblingly away. In an instant Anne put her foot upon it, not too heavily. Frances could see the struggling, swimming movement of the little pink hands of the brute, the twisting and twitching of its pointed nose, as it wrestled under the sole of the boot.

'It *does* wriggle!' said the bonny girl, knitting her brows in a frown at the eerie sensation. Then she bent down to look at her trap. Frances could now see, beyond the edge of the boot-sole, the heaving of the velvet shoulders, the pitiful turning of the sightless face, the frantic rowing of the flat, pink hands.

'Kill the thing,' she said, turning away her face.

'Oh – I'm not,' laughed Anne, shrinking. 'You can, if you like.'

'I *don't* like,' said Frances, with quiet intensity.

After several dabbing attempts, Anne succeeded in picking up the little animal by the scruff of its neck. It threw back its head, flung its long blind snout from side to side, the mouth open in a peculiar oblong, with tiny pinkish teeth at the edge. The blind, frantic mouth gaped and writhed. The body, heavy and clumsy, hung scarcely moving.

'Isn't it a snappy little thing,' observed Anne, twisting to avoid the teeth.

'What are you going to do with it?' asked Frances sharply.

'It's got to be killed – look at the damage they do. I s'll take it home and let dadda or somebody kill it. I'm not going to let it go.'

She swaddled the creature clumsily in her pocket-handkerchief and sat down beside her sister. There was an interval of silence, during which Anne combated the efforts of the mole."

"But at this juncture the mole almost succeeded in wriggling clear. It wrestled and twisted frantically, waved its pointed blind head, its mouth standing open like a little shaft, its big, wrinkled hands spread out.

'Go in with you!' urged Anne, poking the little creature with her forefinger, trying to get it back into the handkerchief. Suddenly the mouth turned like a spark on her finger.

'Oh!' she cried, 'he's bit me.'

She dropped him to the floor. Dazed, the blind creature fumbled round. Frances felt like shrieking. She expected him to dart away in a flash, like a mouse, and there he remained groping; she wanted to cry to him to be gone. Anne, in a sudden decision of wrath, caught up her sister's walking-cane. With one blow the mole was dead. Frances was startled and shocked. One moment the little wretch was fussing in the heat, and the next it lay like a little bag, inert and black – not a struggle, scarce a quiver.

'It is dead!' Frances said breathlessly."

The most revealing poem, by John Clare (1793–1864), "The Mole Catcher," is quoted in Chapter 11, where among other things he describes the same trap as was used by Arthur Randell's father at the beginning of the twentieth century. Aldous Huxley, in the *Burning Wheel* (1916), has a poem called simply "Mole," but this is a greater contribution to literature than to natural history. There are many other poems purporting to be about moles, which use the animal to symbolise some buried facet of man's personality or to illustrate some other fancy of the author without illuminating the life of the animal itself.

Moles, moleskins and parts of moles have been used in various ways. No doubt they played their part in witchcraft and in rural medicine, but the only well-established use appears to be the custom, still practised to-day in the fens, of carrying the dried front feet as a preventive against rheumatism. Skins were, until recently, carried by plumbers and used for wiping joints in pipes. The main use, however, was of the fur, and a good specimen, known as a "Best Winter Clear," brought in as much as 3s. 6d. in 1900. This was a larger sum than might be earned by a full day's work. I know a cottage in the fens built entirely by the sum earned on the side by a farmworker who was also a skilled mole-catcher. It seems a pity that the skins are no longer used, for if as many of the animals are killed (by poison) as ever, moleskins might be a form of adornment not greatly to be criticised by conservationists.

CHAPTER 2

THE ANATOMY OF THE MOLE

THE first time he handles a mole, the average person remarks on its smallness. For some reason, perhaps because he has witnessed the large amount of soil that can be excavated to produce molehills in a few hours, he expects the animal to be considerably larger. The average male mole is about $5\frac{3}{4}$ inches (14.3 cm) long and weighs nearly a quarter of a pound (110 gm). The female is slightly smaller, on the average only $5\frac{1}{4}$ inches (13.4 cm) long and weighing a little over 3 oz (85 gm). The largest mole recorded in Britain weighed nearly 5 oz (133 gm); this was a male. Somewhat larger animals (up to 154 gm) have been found in the Netherlands. The lengths recorded here are from the tip of the snout to the base of the tail, which, if included, adds a further $1\frac{1}{4}$ to $1\frac{1}{2}$ inches (just over 3 cm) to these figures.

Scientists working on moles have made numerous measurements of the size and weight of the animals, and have correlated their findings with the habitats occupied by the population being studied. In general they found larger moles where the food was plentiful. However, some of these findings are of doubtful significance. The measurements of length, provided that only adults are included, may be significant, but the weights are of less value. This is because the weight of an individual may fluctuate so greatly. As is shown in Chapter 6, a hungry mole may consume over half an ounce (15 gm) of food in a few minutes, and increase its weight accordingly. This meal may be digested, and its waste excreted, in a few hours, when the weight may again decrease by nearly 20 per cent. When moles are trapped, some have full stomachs and some empty, and this factor has the greatest effect on the body weight. In comparing sizes, it is best to use starving body weights.

The main characters may be noted in Figure 1. The pink,

FIG. 1 The mole. The eyes of the mole are generally invisible as they are covered by the fur, and the tail is upright to keep contact with the tunnel roof. Thus, its tail is of more value to it than sight in its direction finding.

hairless, pig-like snout is to some extent erectile, and in a dead animal is not so prominent as in life. There is a characteristic pattern of bristles around the snout and on other parts of the body; their sensory function is discussed in Chapter 3. There is no external ear, and the eyes, which are tiny, only measuring about a twenty-fifth of an inch (1 mm) in diameter, can only be seen if the fur on the face is blown back. The mole appears to have no neck (though as in other mammals there are seven cervical vertebrae) and the shoulders are immensely powerful. The forelimbs are adapted for digging; the hind limbs are not so modified. The sesamoid bone arising from the wrist of the front foot acts almost like a sixth finger, and makes the hand broader, more rigid and shovel-like. The tail is club-shaped, being narrower at the base than farther up, and this shape makes it a convenient site to fit a marking ring (see p. 81). In life the tail may be carried erect. The fur is short and silky, with no special direction of "set," so that it can be stroked in any direction.

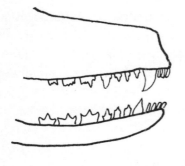

FIG. 2 The teeth of the mole.

25mm

The mole has forty-four teeth, and the dental formula is $\frac{3.1.4.3.}{3.1.4.3.}$. This means that in the top jaw there are three incisors, one canine, four premolars and three molars on each side, while the lower jaw has three incisors, one canine, four premolars and three molars. These teeth are shown in Figure 2. In the upper jaw the incisors are small, and the canine, which is unusual in possessing a double root, is very prominent. The front three premolars are small with a single cusp, the fourth is much larger. The three molars are normal. In the lower jaw the three incisors are small, as is the canine, which in fact looks like a fourth incisor. What looks like a canine tooth is the first premolar. The remaining three premolars and the three molars are normal. Although, as related in D. H. Lawrence's story in Chapter 1, the mole can bite so as to draw blood from man, the teeth are not sufficiently large, nor can the mouth be opened wide enough, for more than a painful "nip" to be inflicted. Nevertheless, it is wise to handle living moles wearing gloves. The age of a mole may be assessed, as is indicated in Chapter 4, by the amount of wear of the teeth.

As has been already mentioned, the shoulders are very powerful. The skeleton is adapted to give attachment to the enlarged muscles, particularly the *Teres major*, and to allow the rotation of the humerus. An interesting adaptation is the keel-shaped foremost joint of the breastbone, to which important muscles are attached. Figure 3 of the skeleton shows the modifications of the bones of the arm and shoulder girdle. A detailed description of the working of the limbs is given in the paper by D. W. Yalden included in the Bibliography (p. 152).

Though the musculature and skeleton of the mole have been admirably described in D. W. Yalden's and other works, the internal organs of the mole, other than the genitalia, seem to have been neglected. Figure 4 is of a general dissection of a male mole. The arrangement of organs is similar to that in most small mammals, and does not require detailed comments, except with regard to the digestive or alimentary system.

The gut is shown in Figure 4 slightly displaced from its normal position inside the body cavity. In Figure 5 the whole length of the alimentary system is shown, dissected out. The process of digestion has been investigated in the living mole. This was done using a modification of the technique used in investigating gastric and peptic ulcers and other digestive

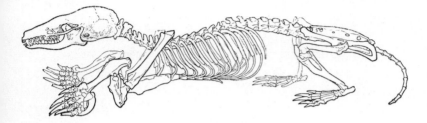

FIG. 3 Skeleton of the mole.

troubles in man, and I am indebted greatly to Mr R. K. Medd
of the Huntingdon Research Centre for collaboration. A commercial preparation of 100 per cent stable dispersion of Barium
Sulphate B.P. was used. This was injected with a hypodermic
syringe, the needle having a rounded end, through the anus
into the gut of large earthworms, *Lumbricus terrestris*. Worms so
treated were readily eaten by moles, which were then examined
by X-ray at quarter-hour intervals for one hour, and then at
half-hour intervals until the barium meal had been voided. The
photographs during the first hour showed rather diffusely the
outline of the stomach, very much as in Figure 4. At the end
of the hour the shadow passed out of the stomach into the small
intestine, and the stomach seemed quite empty within an hour
and a half of the mole's consuming the worms. By this time the
whole length of the small intestine could be distinguished. At
the end of two hours a much clearer picture of the small intestine could be distinguished, as if the gut contents had become
more concentrated. By three and a half hours the small intestine was empty, and the hind gut was clearly shown: the
absorption of water from the gut had markedly concentrated
the barium. By four hours from feeding, defecation, with

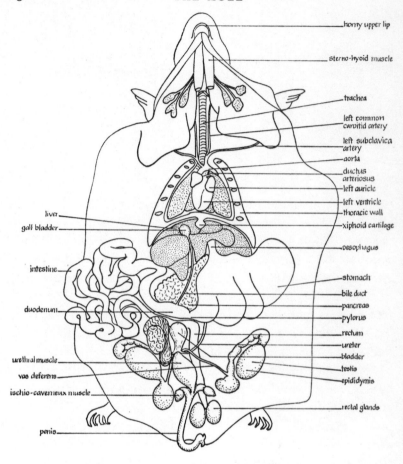

horny upper lip

sterno-hyoid muscle

trachea

left common carotid artery

left subclavica artery

aorta

ductus arteriosus

left auricle

left ventricle

thoracic wall

xiphoid cartilage

oesophagus

liver

gall bladder

stomach

bile duct

pancreas

pylorus

intestine

rectum

ureter

bladder

testis

duodenum

epididymis

urethral muscle

vas deferens

ischio-caverneux muscle

rectal glands

penis

FIG. 4 General dissection of the mole.

typical blackish stools the consistency of toothpaste, began, and the remains of the meal were soon eliminated.

I was surprised at the speed with which the meal passed through the gut. The length of the gut (54 inches, 150 cm) is

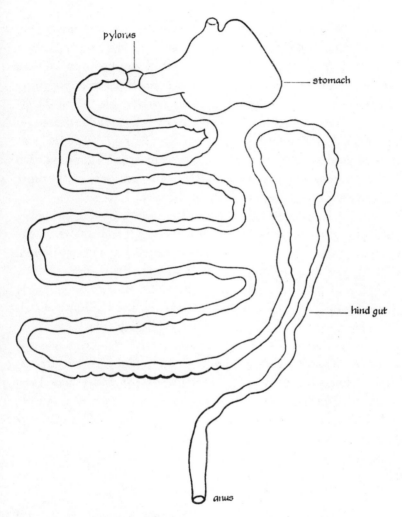

FIG. 5 The alimentary canal of the mole, dissected out.

also longer than I should have expected for a carnivorous animal. Thus a stoat, four times as heavy as a mole, has a gut of only 44 inches (111 cm). Herbivorous animals have very much longer intestines, for instance in a 2½ lb (1 kg) rabbit, 5 yards (4½ metres), and in a tiny vole weighing only half an ounce (15 gm) the gut is two-thirds as long as in a stoat weighing twenty-five times as much. I have no explanation of this difference between moles and other carnivores, though the semi-liquid food arising from a diet consisting largely of earthworms (whose bodies may contain 90 per cent water) may need a longer digestive tract than that which can deal with more concentrated foods like meat from vertebrate prey.

When it is dissected out, the mole's gut appears to be a simple tube of approximately the same diameter all the way from the stomach to the rectum. The pyloric sphincter is well developed, with strong muscles, but no other structures are immediately recognisable. In fact, the large intestine, though not clearly distinguishable in a dissection, appears, when its shape is outlined by a barium shadow in an X-ray photograph, to be about double the diameter of the small intestine which, however, shows no apparent subdivisions in dissection or X-ray examination either. No trace of a caecum or appendix has been detected. Nevertheless, I have no doubt that further research, which is greatly needed, will show many interesting additional features in the mole's digestive system.

CHAPTER 3

SENSE ORGANS

AN animal's sense organs are the means by which it makes contact with the environment. Every animal must record sensations which will enable it to find its food, to escape from enemies, to select a mate, to rear its young, and to do all the other things which make up its life. The stimuli received may contribute to learning, and they may trigger off instinctive reactions.

The mole must therefore have a very adequate series of sense organs, though these may give it a very different picture of its surroundings from that imagined by man, where sight is acute and whose senses of smell and hearing are comparatively feeble. The mole's senses are clearly adequate to allow the animal to colonise a wider range of habitats than almost any other British mammal. Thus we find moles in deciduous and coniferous woodland, in grassland and arable fields, in the peaty soils of the fens below sea-level, in relatively poor moorland soils up to nearly 3,000 feet (900 metres) above sea-level in our mountains, in chalk grassland and the poor sandy soils of the Breckland. The acid peat of upland Britain seems to be the only soil not regularly invaded by moles. This tremendous success of the mole under such a wide range of conditions is something that has not always been realised, and some observers have wrongly thought of it as a poor blind creature dimly aware of what goes on around it and therefore restricted to a limited environment.

In later chapters the mode of life of the mole in these different habitats is discussed. In considering the sense organs, however, some preliminary mention of the mole's habits must be made. We must remember that the mole lives most of its life in underground tunnels, through which it lollops along at up to $2\frac{1}{2}$ miles (4 km) an hour. This is, considering the small size of the animal and the narrowness of the tunnels, a substantial speed, and were it constantly to blunder into the walls it would damage itself, particularly its very sensitive nose which would receive the brunt of the encounter. The mole feeds mainly by picking up worms and arthropods which are found in the burrows, but it also digs new tunnels to increase its feeding area, and any creature discovered as it digs is consumed. Moles have been observed pursuing and catching such agile prey as frogs. Moles leave their burrows and move above ground, and the young in particular may migrate over quite long distances. A mole may find a substantial obstacle (e.g. a live trap, see p. 83) in its burrow, and it may take avoiding action, digging out into untouched soil and making its tunnel in an arc perhaps 2 feet (60 cm) long which takes it accurately back to the existing burrow on the other side. A marked mole may be released up to 200 yards (183 metres) from where it is caught, and makes its way back to the original site within two hours, though it was probably never before near the place of release. During the breeding season a male mole may travel across country for half a mile (a kilometre) in search of a mate. Ordinarily when a mole meets another living animal, including another mole, it attacks it and may kill, or be killed by it, but during the breeding season the sexes maintain a brief truce and pair. We know that all these things happen, but our knowledge of the way the

sense organs work does not by any means fully explain how the
animals cope with all these varied situations.

Those who have studied the mole have expressed different
opinions on its sense of sight, some considering the animal to be
almost or totally blind, others suggesting that it has either true
sight with the ability to perceive definite objects, or at least
that it is able to distinguish light from darkness. The most
thorough investigation of the anatomy and the working of the
eye has been made by T. A. Quilliam and his colleagues. The

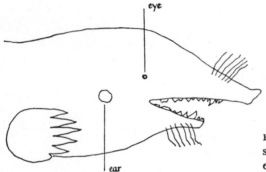

FIG. 6 A mole's head,
showing positions of
eye and ear.

eye is indeed tiny, only one-fortieth of an inch (one millimetre)
in diameter, but it possesses basically all the structures normally
associated with vision in a mammal. Thus it has a conical
cornea, which appears to be transparent. There is an anterior
chamber, filled with clear fluid. The iris has a minute but con-
ventionally-proportioned pupil, which should admit the light
to the lens, which lies just behind this aperture. The lens is
cellular, appearing superficially like that seen in early stages of
embryonic development in some obviously-sighted animals,
where this cellular structure is lost during subsequent develop-

ment to produce the clear glass-like lens of the post-embryonic animal. It has been suggested therefore that the cellular lens indicates that the mole's eye is immature or embryonic. The posterior chamber behind the lens also contains a clear fluid, and the retina, which is richly supplied with nerves, consists of several layers of cells. There are said to be some 100,000 receptors and 4,000 ganglia in the retina (against many million in the eye of a mouse), and the very delicate and thin optic nerve contains only some 200 fibres. A thorough and beautiful description of the anatomy of the eye has been given by T. A. Quilliam.

Notwithstanding the perfection of some of its structures, the small size of the eye and of its optic nerves makes it unlikely that the mole possesses a great degree of visual acuity. Nevertheless, the eye seems to have some function. It has been noted that during activity the eye becomes apparent as it is protruded slightly. However, many of those who have handled live moles are doubtful about its performance. I have never had any reaction by a live mole to a movement, such as passing my hand between the animal and the source of light, when the movement is not accompanied by noise or a draught (two stimuli which we know will affect behaviour). I have flashed a strong electric torch full into a mole's face when it is feeding or seeking for food, with no reaction. In fact, the difference in sensitivity of a mole (with eyes) and an earthworm (only possessing rather simple photoreceptors in its skin) is remarkable. The beam of a torch will cause an earthworm to retreat into its burrow with immense speed, while the mole offers no apparent reaction.

There is evidence, however, that the eye does respond to some visual stimuli. R. D. and J. S. Lund, in Dr Quilliam's laboratory, showed that moles could be taught to discriminate light from dark. In a simple "maze" they taught moles to come to food either at the illuminated or the dark side of the apparatus. However, the light threshold which was detectable was quite a high one, some hundred times greater than the minimum appreciated by the dark-adapted eye in man.

It has been suggested that the ability to distinguish light is important in preventing moles from coming on to the surface during the day. This may sometimes apply, but experience shows that moles do, in fact, come out in daylight, as was recorded by D. H. Lawrence in Chapter 1, and can be frequently observed by anyone working in the field. I believe myself that moles come on the surface by day more often than is commonly believed, and that they do not necessarily come up above ground more frequently during the night. The fact that mole remains are found as often in food pellets of day-flying herons as in those of nocturnal tawny owls supports this contention. It should further be remembered that moles seldom occur in great numbers, and that such small creatures will not easily be seen in grass. It is perhaps surprising that they are seen above ground so frequently. Thus I think that the evidence available suggests that sight is not important to the mole, and that, although it may be able to discriminate between dark and a moderately bright light, even this may have little effect on behaviour.

It is sometimes asked whether the mole's small eye is a primitive feature, or whether degeneration has occurred because of its largely (though not entirely) subterranean life. It has been noted that all insectivores, including shrews and hedgehogs, have rather poor vision, and rely on other senses to a considerable extent. Insectivores are looked upon as being "primitive" mammals, and it is possible that visual acuity was never a feature of this branch of the mammalian stock. The condition in the mole suggests degeneration even from this rather low level of efficiency, in an animal with other senses which fully make up for the loss. Incidentally, a mole closely related to our British species, *Talpa caeca*, found in Spain and southern Europe as far east as Greece, has the eyes covered by skin, and it is therefore believed to be quite blind.

One possible function of the eye is that it detects changes in day length, and that this controls the changes in the sex organs and the onset of breeding (see p. 45). We know that day length has such an effect in many birds and mammals; only experiments on captive moles will show whether the same applies to them.

It has already been noted that the mole has no pinna or external ear; this is presumably an adaptation to life underground. The position of the ear (Fig. 6) can be determined by wetting the fur and manipulating it. The structure of the internal ear is not such as to suggest particularly acute hearing. Thus the cochlea has only $1\frac{3}{4}$ turns, and is perhaps the shortest found in any mammal. In man the cochlea has $2\frac{3}{4}$ turns, in the bat $3\frac{1}{4}$. There may be no definite relationship between these figures and the working of the organ, but this is a subject needing further study. However, there is no doubt that a mole can hear. There are several authentic accounts of captive moles being taught to come to feed when called by the human voice or by ringing a bell, and alarm can be caused by various and not very loud noises.

Animals are usually expected to hear the sounds they themselves make. Moles "twitter" when feeding and when exploring their surroundings. They also emit loud sounds, including high-pitched squeals, when frightened or when fighting. It has been suggested that they may also emit ultrasonic noises, but so far all attempts to detect these have failed. It is also possible that, underground in a burrow, sounds travel as in the old-fashioned "speaking tubes" found in Victorian mansions to communicate between the drawing-room and the servants in the basement, so that in the mole's environment, abnormally acute hearing is not required.

Smell and taste are related senses, stimulated by chemical substances breathed in with the air (smell) or present in the food and drink and detected by receptors in the mouth (taste). In fact, we smell our food at the same time as we taste it, and our reaction depends on the complicated sensations simultaneously received. The mole does not appear to have a very acute sense of smell. It does detect both food and water at distances up to about 2 inches (5 cm). Thus a captive mole will turn to pick up a worm, or to drink from a dish of water, when it is within this distance of the worm or the water. This reaction is not inevitable, and even a hungry mole may sometimes pass very close to food without apparently detecting it. Experience suggests that olfaction is of only limited importance.

Taste in the mole has not been thoroughly studied. Worms are readily eaten at most times by all individuals studied. Meat, either fresh or partially decomposed, is usually taken. Soon after being captured moles are often more "choosey" than they become later, and insects such as mealworms are temporarily rejected. Water and milk are readily drunk, particularly by moles which have been starved or which have had meat rather than worms (which already contain so much water). There are reports of plant food, including cabbage, being eaten, but I have never succeeded in persuading a mole to try such sub-

stances, nor have I found more than fragments of vegetable
matter, which could have been accidentally ingested, in mole
stomachs which I have dissected.

We have so far considered the so-called "special" senses of
vision, hearing, olfaction and taste. It appears likely that the
mole is nearly blind and that the other senses are not particularly well developed. There is so far no indication of how the
mole manages so successfully to overcome the difficulties of
living in a subterranean environment, or of how it is able to
colonise such a wide range of habitats.

This brings us to a consideration of what may be called the
"cutaneous" senses, which include touch and the appreciation
of heat, cold, pain and vibration. In this connection the snout,
and the bristles on various parts of the body and in particular
the face, would seem to be important, though the whole of the
surface of the skin contains sense organs generally of a less
specialised kind.

The pink, hairless snout is covered with thousands of tiny
raised papillae which are richly supplied with nerve endings.
These are known as Eimer's organs. The tip of the snout is
capable of being dilated by means of the blood, and when so
erected it is probable that the Eimer's organs are particularly
sensitive. So far the exact importance of the snout, and of the
stimuli which are detected, has not been elucidated. It can undoubtedly act as a very delicate organ of touch, and it is said
that it is so sensitive that a mole dies immediately if struck on
the tip of the nose. I have not tried such a cruel experiment,
but have noticed that, if the snout is accidentally touched even
gently, the animal reacts as if to pain. It is also possible that
the Eimer's organs detect chemical stimuli (that is, smells).
They may also be "teletactile receptors" and, presumably by

detecting changes in air pressure and minute air currents, they may locate objects at some distance. They may also be affected by temperature and infra-red radiation. I believe that it is likely that the snout does play an important part in determining the way in which a mole perceives its surroundings, and I hope that further research will elucidate this further.

The various vibrissae, particularly those on the face, though some also exist on the tail, are clearly important. They are essentially long hairs with a rich supply of nerve endings around their base. Similar structures in the cat and other mammals exist. They clearly perceive the very slightest touch of a solid object. It seems likely that they can also detect compression waves in the air and help the animals to detect obstacles before running into them.

The pattern of cutaneous sense organs is also complex. An unusual structure is the Pinkus plate, found in the skin of the abdominal region. This is a papilla richly supplied with nerves. The working of these organs also is not yet properly understood.

This account of the sense organs clearly reveals a very unsatisfactory state of affairs. We really do not understand how the mole finds its way about. However, I think that a further study of these unusual cutaneous structures, in particular those of the snout, is likely to demonstrate their importance.

The mole probably also has a well-developed "kinaesthetic sense" which is defined as an imprinted pattern of memory, or a compound of muscle sense and memory (or, possibly, by saying that the animal remembers where it has been). This sense enables us to find the light switch of a bedside lamp in the dark in a familiar room without groping for it. It could enable the mole to avoid bumping into the walls of its winding burrow. This sense is also invoked in explaining how the animal avoids an obstruction and digs around it through untouched soil to find the burrow again, though I do not find this explanation very convincing.

It is tempting to assume that the mole has other and more unusual senses. It has been suggested that it finds its way in its burrows by some sort of "radar," using some type of radiation which we do not experience. It may be hypersensitive to changes in temperature, humidity or atmospheric pressure. It is conceivable that it has other senses to which we have, at present, no clue. There is still a need for a great deal more research in this subject.

actually exceed that found in the male, but this only happens
when the female can be distinguished easily by the presence of
this opening. After the young are born, the female opening
closes again and heals, though a slight scar remains to distinguish the older from the virgin female.

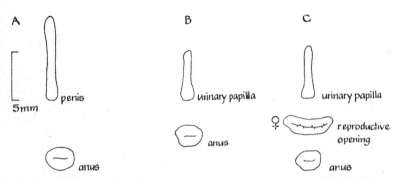

FIG. 7 External genital and excretory organs of the mole. A, male,
B, female outside breeding season. C, female during breeding
season.

The internal sex organs also undergo cyclical changes during
the breeding season. In the male, the testes increase in size
enormously (Fig. 8). Although a young male, born in April,
has reached its adult weight by the end of July, the testes are
still minute, weighing perhaps as little as 10 mg. By September
these have increased somewhat, to a weight of between 200 and
400 milligrames, and they are indistinguishable from the
testes of older males. Examination of sections of testes at this
time indicates that they are in a quiescent state. Late in November cellular changes occur, leading to the production of active
spermatozoa in February and March. The testes also increase
in size, at first slowly, but then suddenly in February they swell

to a maximum weight of 3,000 mg (nearly ⅛ of an ounce), with an average figure in the region of 2,000 mg. The associated structures, including the prostate gland, undergo similar but even more extreme cyclical changes in size.

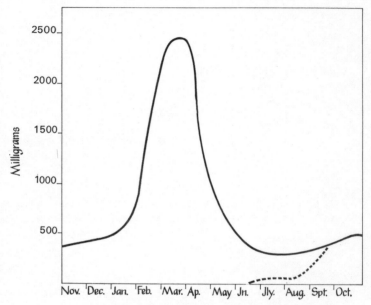

FIG. 8 Weight of male testis in different months.

In the female the greatest differences are noted in the size of the reproductive tract (Fig. 9). In the virgin, and in the older female after the birth of the young, it is very small, measuring only some 20 per cent of the body length and weighing perhaps 50 mg. In the breeding season it expands to 70 per cent of the body length and the weight increases to as much as 450 mg. The ovaries, however, do not swell up as do the testes in the male, as in fact they are smaller during the breeding season than during the rest of the year. However, the part of the ovary which produces the eggs is tiny except in the breeding season; the increase in size during the non-active stage is due to the proliferation of the interstitial gland, an organ which forms part of the ovary and whose function has not yet been elucidated.

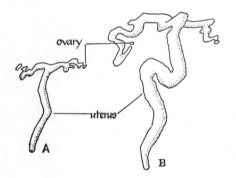

FIG. 9 Internal female reproductive organs: A, outside breeding season. B, during breeding season.

It has been suggested by V. C. Wynne Edwards that this proliferation of the interstitial cells causes the ovary to have an endocrine function similar to that of the inactive male testis, and that this accounts for the similarity in behaviour of the two sexes outside the breeding season. If this is so, the countrymen who say that "all moles are males" for most of the year, may not have been so far wrong, at least from the physiological and psychological points of view.

We have now described the anatomical changes which occur in early spring and which make pairing and reproduction possible. There is no apparent change in the behaviour of the female, which remains in the area she has inhabited during the winter. The males, however, are more obviously affected.

Studies made of males marked with radioactive rings (see p. 86) show that, in many cases, the animals behave throughout the winter in the same way as the females, remaining in one circumscribed area. In February and March, however, they may move considerable distances, up to half a mile (a kilometre) in search of a mate. They may travel through existing tunnel systems if these exist, as they may in a wood on clay soil, or in old pasture which has not recently been disturbed. They may dig a new burrow; we have no idea how they navigate with the hope of finding a female. They may also move mainly above ground. It was suggested that the ardent moles constructed a special type of burrow when searching for females. This was called the "trace d'amour" and was described as a straight cutting with no roof, directed to the nearest female territory. The idea was that the male had not time to dig a proper tunnel and compromised on this more easily excavated trench. Although we do find this type of open-topped burrow, it seems to be constructed at other times (e.g. at the interface with snow and the soil) and not specifically as an aid to mating.

There is no doubt that the male's behaviour is changed during the breeding season. I have never succeeded in keeping an animal in captivity for any length of time during that period; it seems likely that confinement becomes intolerable and the animals die from "frustration."

I have found no account of copulation in the scientific literature. I once said this in a lecture, and the matter was commented in a popular newspaper. This occurred while Arthur Randell was writing *Fenland Molecatcher*, and it caused him to comment:

"A scientist was reported, not long ago, to have said that

little or nothing is known of the mating habits of moles; I can assure him, however, that I have seen the sexual act performed by the animals and could give him a detailed description of it."

I had not yet met Mr Randell when he wrote this, but we did meet soon after and he kept his promise. He told me that when he was a boy of about ten, he was out with his father trapping moles, when he came across two moles above the ground. Instead of fighting, these appeared to be quite friendly to one another, and one mounted the other in a manner described as similar to that adopted by dogs when pairing. At this moment Mr Randell's father came up, and being a typical Victorian, he suitably admonished his innocent son for witnessing such a spectacle. Mr Randell tells me that he has seen copulation on possibly two other occasions during his seventy years of studying the mole. On all occasions the animals have been above the ground. If, in fact, someone as skilful in studying the mole has only seen this act so infrequently in a lifetime of acute observation, it is not surprising that others of us, with less experience, have so far missed it. Also we do not know whether pairing above ground is normal, or whether these were exceptional encounters and that copulation is usually performed in the dark privacy of the burrow.

Some observations by A. J. B. Rudge support the latter view. He marked several moles of both sexes with radio-active rings, as described in Chapter 7, and followed their movements underground using a Geiger counter. Though he could not see the moles, he knew where they were, and could hear them if they squealed. On one occasion when the two sexes met sounds as of fighting were heard, and the male retreated rapidly. On another day in March a male entered a female's territory and approached her. No sounds suggesting fighting were heard. The two animals then apparently entered a nearby nest and remained together for over an hour. The female was captured soon afterwards when a vaginal smear showed the presence of sperm, so copulation must have recently occurred.

Attempts to pair moles in captivity have, as far as I know, always failed. Captive moles will always fight, often to the death, and at most times of year sex does not affect this behaviour. It has been suggested that the female may only be on heat for a few hours, and that this may affect her reaction to the male and his response. Nevertheless, as practically every female caught during the appropriate season is pregnant, the mechanisms to ensure meeting and pairing are clearly effective. This is obviously a field for further research.

Gestation lasts for four weeks. The young are born in mid-April in southern and eastern England, a week or two later in Wales and in Scotland. However, irregularities in this pattern may occur. In 1964 severe floods affected the fens in Huntingdonshire at the end of March. In Monks Wood itself the higher ground escaped flooding; here all female moles captured in early April were pregnant. Woodwalton Fen was deeply covered with water for a few days and the moles were driven out. When the water retreated they returned, but trapping soon after (when the animals in the nearby wood were pregnant) revealed none with embryos. Whether the flood had caused abortion or resorption of the embryos we do not know. In this case normal pregnancies did occur, a month later than in unflooded areas nearby.

The mammary glands, which extend subcutaneously on to the back of the female, thicken and spread during the last week of gestation. There are four pairs of nipples, two pairs on the chest and two on the abdomen. This suggests that eight young could be suckled, but half this number is usual. Between three and seven embryos have been found by dissection, but here again the average number is four, and there is comparatively little ante-natal mortality.

I can find no record of young being successfully reared in captivity. I have never yet succeeded in catching alive a pregnant female and getting her to settle down in confinement, but I am sure that this will eventually prove the method the most likely to succeed. The following account by Frank G. Reeman appeared in *The Countryman* in 1964 and indicated that when disturbed moles may not be good mothers.

"We were wandering through a strip of woodland one afternoon in May when we noticed a rustling among dead leaves. I cleared a circle round the spot with a stick and poked about until a mole made a break for freedom, and I was able to catch her. We installed her in a rabbit-hutch, filled the nest compartment with a box of firm soil and covered the floor of the other half also with a layer, joining the two with a small wire-netting tunnel; and we added a little hay for bedding. To our surprise the mole proved docile and adaptable; she soon learned to come scuttling along the 'run' when we rattled the food tin, and she took worms from our fingers. If stroked, she stopped eating only long enough to remove the offending finger with an upward thrust of one forefoot. She was rather less than $3\frac{1}{4}$ oz and ate more than her own weight of worms on the first day. That posed a problem, because there had been no rain for weeks and the soil was dry; but she would accept lean raw beef as a substitute, having first finished off the few worms we provided. Three or four days after her capture we opened the soil box to find two tiny pink moles on the surface, one with its head bitten off; the other we removed and kept warm. When we put the mother on the grass, she sniffed around, accepted a worm and then started to chase her tail, uttering low-pitched yelps. We saw she was giving birth to a third baby, assisting delivery with her muzzle. When she had cleaned the pink and wrinkled offspring she nudged it, but it did not respond. She then cleaned herself, nosed the baby again and, when it failed to move, bit off its head and turned to burrow in the earth. We fed the remaining young one at intervals with glucose on a fine brush; it could burrow effectively between the fingers of a tightly clenched hand but died after eleven hours. Would the mother have reared it, if we had left it with her? We were afraid that, in captivity, she would mutilate it with her sharp teeth, as she had the others. She stayed with us for two months after the birth, lively and in good health, until one night the cage door was not fastened and she slipped away."

Nests containing young have often been found in the field. These nests are filled with dry grass or leaves, collected from above ground. The process of collecting leaves was described many years ago by Owen Jones as follows:

"I heard a rustling quite near me. I thought it must be a mouse . . . Another rustle, and I saw a dead oak-leaf move. I sank on my knees and crawled to the spot. Within a yard of my face I saw the pinky snout of a mole: never was more than the snout and head . . . to be seen: its body remained on one of those shallow surface-runs. With amazing swiftness the snout felt all round, and each dry leaf within reach would be grabbed and drawn under: in about ten seconds the mole would return. When there were no more leaves within reach of one opening, the mole would thrust through the surface in a fresh place, and continue its leaf-gathering with incredible energy."

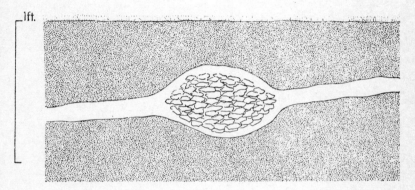

FIG. 10 The mole's nest.

Gillian Godfrey has made the fullest study of mole breeding, including marking mother and some young with radioactive rings. At birth the young are tiny, pink, hairless creatures, weighing only $\frac{1}{8}$ oz (3.5 gm) and measuring $1\frac{1}{2}$ inches (35 mm) long. They grow rapidly, and in three weeks are not far short of adult size. The coat covers the body by the seventeenth day, and the eyes open on the twenty-second. The young are entirely milk fed for at least a month, when they begin to leave the nest but the young and the mother remain together for another two or three weeks. During the early days if the young are disturbed the mother will carry them away to another nest, perhaps some distance away. The mother remains with the young during her resting periods, but may leave them for two hours or more when she herself is searching for food. During this period the body temperature of the young moles falls many degrees; they are evidently essentially poikilothermic for the first days after birth. Young moles, fully or almost fully grown, remain amicably in each other's company during this period. Thus D. T. Edmed of Hastings, after taking me to task for a statement reported in the press that two moles fight to the death, writes as follows:

> "Early this summer (1968) I was on the South Downs working out a ramble for my local club. I had strayed from the footpath somewhat. It was a very hot afternoon. I heard a rustling noise ahead and moved quietly forward. Two moles were apparently sun-bathing! They were not at all hostile. I was amazed to see two together and also to see a mole at all in the hot sunshine. (It was about 2.45 p.m.) They *appeared* to be rolling on their backs enjoying the sun, but as they had heard me they disappeared quickly into the thick grass at the bottom of the wire fence. They were side-by-side about 4–6 inches apart when I saw them."

Many other observers also report amicable encounters in early summer.

Most moles are born in underground nests lined with grass or leaves, but some are found in fortresses. The construction of the fortress is one of the mysteries in the life of the mole. Molehills are usually structureless piles of earth, the spoil removed in digging a burrow. Occasionally, however, an enormous hill, perhaps up to 3 feet (1 metre) high is found. This differs from a molehill not only in size but also in containing one or more nests and a series of burrows. Most fortresses in April contain young. Fortresses appear most frequent in areas liable to flooding and are said to indicate preparation for such an event, but even in the fens only a tiny proportion, at most one in twenty, of moles makes a fortress, the rest having ordinary underground nests. We also occasionally find a genuine fortress on high ground which is never flooded. It is sometimes suggested in the literature that every mole makes a fortress. This is certainly not the case; we also have no idea why a small proportion of moles behave so differently from their fellows.

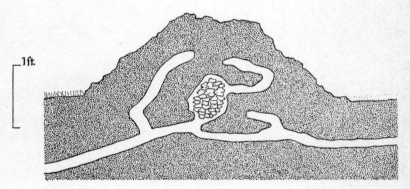

FIG. 11 The mole's fortress.

I know of no successful attempts to rear young moles taken from the nest. There are no data for the composition of mole milk, but many small animals produce a rather concentrated fluid richer than cow's milk. I have tried to feed a mole about two days old with evaporated milk from a pipette. The creature fed readily at two-hourly intervals and survived for three days, but only increased very slightly in weight. I evidently did not use the proper formula.

Moles normally have only one litter a year, but occasionally

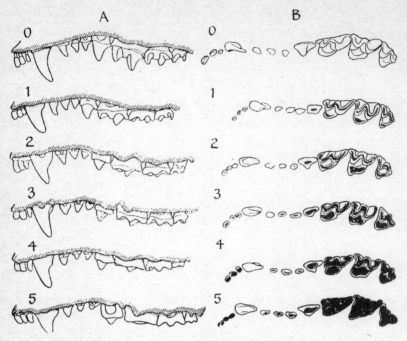

FIG. 12 Tooth wear in moles of different ages. A, lateral view of upper jaw; B, ventral view of upper jaw.

(in perhaps 3 per cent of individuals) a second one is produced later in the summer. It has been suggested that autumn litters represent precocious breeding by first-year females, but this has not been established.

After leaving the mother, many young moles migrate to find a territory, moving above ground. During this period they are often taken as prey by predatory birds, and are also found squashed by traffic on roads. By autumn most of the survivors are established underground, where they are safe from most predators.

Attempts have been made to discover how long most moles live. It is simple to recognise juveniles during the first summer by examining the testis size in males and the absence of the genital aperture (or of the scar which marks its position) in the female. For others than juveniles, age is determined by studying the wear of the teeth. Fig. 12 is from the work of I. Grülich, who studied large numbers of these animals. Investigations in late summer have shown a mole population to contain about 45 per cent of juveniles, 40 per cent of one–two-year-olds, and the remainder of older animals reaching to a small minority with a maximum age of five years. The causes of death of these older moles are not known.

CHAPTER 5

FOOD

ALMOST all accounts of moles start by saying that they are very voracious, eating their own weight (or sometimes twice their own weight) of food every twenty-four hours. Many investigations have said that if they are starved for even as short a period as four hours they perish. Finally, they say that moles dig almost incessantly in their search for food. Unfortunately none of these three statements is true. Nevertheless, they are based on some sort of observation, for if a mole is captured and put into a bucket of soil with a substantial number of worms as food, it will be heard digging frantically for a few hours and then it will probably be found dead on the surface. However, it will not have died directly of starvation but because it has not been able to adapt to its unfamiliar surroundings. A bucket full of loose earth is not a suitable habitat.

The first thing that must be realised is that a mole does most of its feeding when it is running along existing burrows. These act as a sort of "pit-fall trap," into which worms and insects blunder and are picked up and eaten. Burrowing is done to increase the size of the feeding area rather than in an immediate attempt to find food. However, moles do sometimes feed above ground, collecting insects, slugs and worms by nosing about among grass and litter. They also feed when they are making superficial tunnels pushed through the upper part of sandy or other fairly easily worked soil.

The diet of moles has been studied mainly by the dissection and examination of stomach contents. Many workers have made such studies, in different countries and different habitats. It is difficult to obtain strictly quantitative data from these dissections, as when a mole is trapped we cannot tell how recently it has fed. It seems likely that some sorts of food, for instance earthworms or slugs, will be more quickly rendered down into an unrecognisable slush than will hard-bodied insects whose consumption is therefore likely to be exaggerated. Worms which are swallowed whole or in large pieces may be recognisable if found soon enough after ingestion, but the complete absence of records of vertebrate material ("meat") from stomachs may mean that these simply have not been recognised.

Gillian Godfrey examined the stomachs of some 700 moles from Suffolk fenland in eastern England. Some of these were from arable fields, others from pasture. The main constituent was earthworm material, but a high proportion also contained both larval and adult insects. However, while the worms contributed as much as 8,000 mg to a fairly full stomach, few contained as much as 100 mg of insects, though very large numbers of tiny insects were sometimes present. Small amounts of vegetable matter were discovered in a few moles, but they appeared to have been ingested accidentally. A small number (about 2 per cent) of stomachs contain "stomach stones." These may be over half an inch (1.2 cm) long and consist of compressed indigestible materials, mainly of grass or other plant material, but also including mole fur and mineral material. The significance of these stones is not known. I do not think they have any real resemblance to the pellets of fur, bone, etc. produced by owls and hawks, nor is there any evidence that

they are voided as are these pellets. Some are indeed too big
to be able to pass up the oesophagous.

J. Oppermann has studied the diet of moles from grassland,
deciduous woodland and pine-forest near Berlin. He found a
vast predominance of earthworms in moles from grassland and
from deciduous woodland, but that insects predominated (in
mass as well as in numbers) in those from pine forest. A surprising discovery was of pieces of truffle (Ascomycetes) in 30
per cent of moles from pine forests. This is the only well-
authenticated case suggesting that a vegetable food was commonly consumed. Perhaps the mole is more of a gourmet than
is generally recognised!

I deal in more detail with the food from different habitats in
Chapter 8. For the moment it suffices to note that earthworms
have usually been found to be the most important constituent
in those habitats where they form the greatest part of the biomass of the soil fauna.

As well as forming the most common element in the diet,
surplus worms are collected and stored. There are many old
reports of this custom; thus Edward Jesse, writing in 1853, says:
"The following observation was made by a crown mole-catcher
in Richmond Park: 'A sort of basin of clay is made, as a de-
pository for worms. The basin will sometimes contain almost a
peck of worms, bitten near the head but not killed. This may
be a way of obtaining a constant supply of worms without the
moles moving far away from their young during spring. The
young are very tender and need much warmth from their
parents'." Except for the assumption about the "parents" (we
have seen that it is only the mother who cares for the young)
this would seem to be an accurate picture, as was confirmed
when worm stores were scientifically investigated by A. C.

Evans at Rothamsted. He found that these stores consisted almost entirely of one species, *Lumbricus terrestris*. This is spoken of as "the common earthworm," though surveys have shown that other species occur in larger numbers. It is, however, the commonest *large* earthworm to be found in worked soil such as a vegetable garden or arable field. Nevertheless, the mole must exhibit considerable selectivity in choosing its stores. The largest collection investigated contained no fewer than 115 specimens of this species. They all had had their front end damaged or bitten off, and experiments showed that worms so injured lived without losing much weight, and that they remained in much the same place for some two months until they had regenerated the lost segments. Thus the stores would be available for a long time, though we do not know whether moles always find these stores in times of food shortage. Perhaps, like the nuts buried by squirrels, they are often lost.

Captive moles will also store surplus food. When a mole is given a worm, this is seized by the front feet and is run through the feet in a manner similar to that which would be adopted in climbing up a rope. When the head is reached, this is bitten, and the worm is then consumed from head to tail in a matter of seconds even with a large *L. terrestris* weighing $\frac{1}{4}$ oz (6 gm). Sometimes the mole gets the worm the wrong way round and ends up with the tail; this is seldom bitten, and the process is reversed so that the worm's head is eventually presented and consumed in the normal manner. A hungry mole will eat several worms in this way, up to a total weight of about 12 gm. The next worm is treated in the same way, and its head is usually bitten. Most observers have assumed that this worm, and the next, and the next is also eaten, hence the belief that the mole is a gourmand (as well as, possibly, a gourmet!). However, careful observation will show that many of the worms which are apparently "eaten" are, in fact, taken away and cached in a corner of the box. In nature only worms have been found in food stores, but in captivity mealworms or baby mice are treated in the same way.

There are numerous reports of worms fleeing on to the surface when a mole is burrowing in the vicinity. Sometimes birds have been seen to congregate to feed on the escaping worms. There are also accounts of the mole coming up on to the surface in pursuit, and of catching and eating these worms itself.

In captivity moles have been kept alive on beef steak, heart, liver and also on baby mice. It was reported that they would eat some ten or twelve new-born mice (nearly an ounce in total weight) in a day, and store any more that were provided, eating them the next day if their ration was reduced. Surplus insect larvae such as mealworms are also stored, but they are not immobilised and soon escape. If this happens to insects in the wild, it would account for their not being discovered in stores.

Wild moles undoubtedly eat carrion. I have found dead birds partially dragged into a burrow and the breast muscles consumed. There are stories told by gamekeepers of moles burrowing under pheasant nests and taking the eggs and chicks, but they need to be confirmed before being accepted.

The most remarkable feat is that of catching and eating a frog. This was reported as long ago as 1899, by H. Rider Haggard in *A Farmer's Year*, an account of agricultural and social conditions in East Anglia. A very similar account was written in 1968 by Captain H. D. Nichol, R.N., Retd, and published in *Country Life*, as follows:

"One evening in early autumn some years ago I was walking in a grass field close along the side of a little wood hoping for a rabbit. Suddenly a large frog emerged from the wood, going at a good pace in long hops and closely pursued by a mole, which was hunting it like a spaniel, though whether by scent, sight or sound was not apparent. In four or five yards it caught the frog, turned it over on its back and, holding it down with its great spade-like fore feet, started eating its stomach while the poor victim kicked and struggled in vain. This all happened right in front of me and only a few feet away."

If an agile animal like a frog can be successfully hunted in this way, moles may sometimes also chase young birds or mice.

As indicated above, I believe that the capacity for food of the mole has been greatly exaggerated. I kept a mole under observation for all its waking hours for five days, using the technique described in Chapter 7. I gave it as many earthworms as it would actually consume, and found that during each period of twenty-four hours it took 47, 51, 47, 54 and 46 gm (mean consumption 49 gm). The weight of the mole varied between 87 and 102 gm during this period, depending on the fullness of its stomach, but the starved weight (87 gm) was reasonably maintained. This indicated that the animal was satisfied with half its body weight of worms. However, even this is something of an overestimate. When a mole feeds on a worm, it discards part of its prey, particularly the gut if this contains soil. Thus if a mole consumes worms weighing 15 gm, its increase in body weight may be only 12 gm.

Other foods are eaten in even smaller quantities. I have never been able to persuade a mole to take more than 20 gm (less than a quarter of its weight) of mealworms in twenty-four hours. These contain more fat and less water than worms. Similarly, the amount of steak or liver actually consumed, even when unlimited amounts are available, is of the same order.

I made one experiment to discover the minimum requirements of a mole. In this I cut down the amount of food supplied and noted the changes in the starved body weight. When only 10 gm of worms or meat were provided, the starved weight remained constant and there were no symptoms of starvation. Even 5 gm seemed to be reasonably adequate. The mole survived a period of twenty-four hours without food on several occasions. During this period the starved weight fell only by about 5 gm, though, as has already been mentioned, the gross weight could fall by 15 gm during the first four hours after a meal. When allowed access to food, the starved mole soon recovered its previous weight. I have not deliberately starved moles to death, but I know of others who have found that when feeding has been overlooked at week-ends forty-eight hours seems to be about the maximum period that can be endured without food.

These experiments were made with moles which had "settled down" in captivity. When newly caught they are often hyperactive and difficult to study. The behaviour pattern soon becomes very similar to that found in the wild in those which survive (see p. 90). Field observations on moles living in areas with a very poor soil fauna (p. 99) also confirm the finding that the animal's appetite has been overestimated.

In Chapter 6 the periodic activity and feeding of moles is more fully described. Briefly this may be summarised by saying that moles usually have three periods of rest, and three of

1. *Above*, a mole which has come out of its burrow to search for food among dead leaves. *Below*, a mole eating an earthworm.

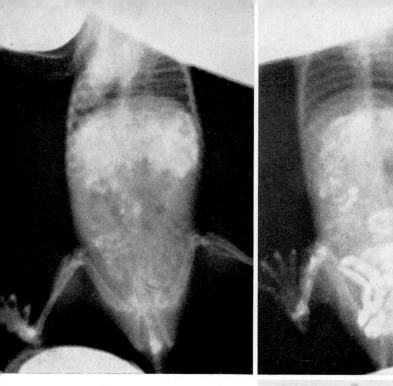

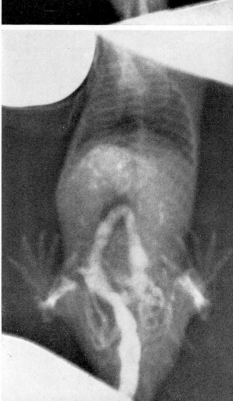

2. X-ray photographs of a mole which has eaten worms containing barium, to give a shadow of the gut contents. These pictures should be compared with Fig. 4 (page 30), showing the gut in a dissection. *Top left*, Immediately after feeding. The stomach is shown in outline. The picture is not very clear because the barium is mixed with a lot of worm tissue. *Top right*, 2½ hours after feeding. The meal has reached the small intestine. Some water has been extracted during digestion, so the outline is clearer. *Below*, 3½ hours after feeding. The meal has passed right along the gut to the hind gut and rectum. Defaecation has begun.

activity, every twenty-four hours. I was surprised to find that a starved mole followed the same pattern as one with unlimited food. This is clearly a useful adaptation to its way of life. If a mole runs along its burrow system and finds insufficient food, the best plan is for it to go and rest and conserve its resources, as during this rest period more worms or insects may enter the burrows and be available for consumption at the next active period. Digging to extend the run is usually done early in the active period, when the animal is still "fresh."

There is some uncertainty about the importance of drinking in the life of the mole. In captivity moles drink water readily if they are starved, or if they have been fed on comparatively dry foods like meat or mealworms. A mole can detect water at a distance and turns sharply in its path to find a dish and drinks from it. A starved mole will fill its stomach full by consuming some 15 cc (over half a fluid ounce) of water in about three minutes. It will climb half in to a shallow dish of water and drink from its surface. It is also easily taught to take water from the type of patent drinking fountain used for pet mice. There seems no doubt that to drink is a natural reaction, and one that is performed most efficiently. The trouble is that in the wild, water does not seem to be readily available under the conditions where it is most required. It is true that where a stream runs through a meadow, burrows may run down to it, and many moles may be caught in these runs, giving the impression that they are used by many animals seeking water. However, such habitats are usually rich in earthworms, which should themselves give sufficient water to make further drinking unnecessary. In dry regions with few worms, where insects form the greater part of the diet, no water may be available within the range of the moles. It is suggested that under these circumstances moles may come on to the surface to lap the dew, but this, though likely, is still only supposition.

The state of nutrition of an animal may affect its growth. Moles vary considerably in adult size and in weight. Conclusions from individual weights must be drawn with caution, fluctuations caused by the fullness or emptiness of the stomach may give rise to rapid changes of 10–15 per cent. However, the following figures for mole weights from different habitats are interesting.

Table 1

WEIGHTS OF MOLES FROM DIFFERENT HABITATS

***** = very plentiful food, * = food sparse. Intermediate numbers of * indicate comparative plentifulness.

Habitat	Weight		Food	Author
	♂	♀		
Monks Wood (Deciduous woodland)	97.7	84.5	*****	K.M.
Woodwalton Fen (Peat)	106.2	81.1	**	K.M.
Breckland (Sandy soil)	94.5	81.5	*	K.M.
Suffolk farmland (Peat)	110.0	85.4	***	Godfrey
Berlin (Meadow)	103.0	84.5	****	Oppermann
Berlin (Deciduous wood)	92.0	71.5	****	Oppermann
Berlin (Pine forest)	77.0	64.0	**	Oppermann
Netherlands (New Polder)	122.0	93.0	***	Haeck

These figures show that the smallest moles came from the Berlin coniferous forests, where the food was sparse. However,

in Britain, there seems no such correlation. In my own experience, the Monks Wood moles from the most productive habitat
were not significantly heavier than those from the Breck. The
most outstanding figures are those from the New Polders in the
Netherlands, where the moles are enormous. Their heaviest
male actually weighed 154 gm, a far greater weight than
recorded elsewhere. This difference is much bigger than any
fluctuation due to stomach content. The polders yield a sufficient food supply, but much lower than that in many British
habitats. It would be interesting to find if there is perhaps a
special Dutch race or sub-species of *Talpa europaea*.

CHAPTER 6

DIGGING AND BUILDING

As we have seen, the mole is anatomically adapted to be able to dig. Its front feet form broad, rigid shovels, and these are moved by immensely powerful muscles attached to strong arm, breast and shoulder bones. If a live mole is dropped on to any but the hardest surface, it buries itself in a few seconds.

Everyone is familiar with the piles of earth created by the tunnelling activities of the mole. These molehills, heaps or tumps, are the spoil expelled from the burrows dug under the ground. The actions of the mole in digging its burrows, and in expelling the spoil, are of considerable interest.

Only the front feet are used in digging. When an animal digs itself in from the surface, a sort of "breast stroke" action is used. The front feet are brought together, and then they are thrust sideways, tearing a hole in the turf. The snout is now thrust into the cavity, care being taken to avoid damaging its delicate surface. A further breast stroke is then made, allowing the animal to move farther into the ground, and the action is rapidly repeated until the whole body disappears. In very soft soil, the same "swimming" action may continue, producing a shallow run with no spoil to be pushed up into molehills (Fig. 13). A ridge on the surface indicates the position of the run.

These surface runs, with no molehills, are frequently made, particularly in newly-cultivated arable fields, or in sandy and peaty soils. The essential condition is that the earth is soft

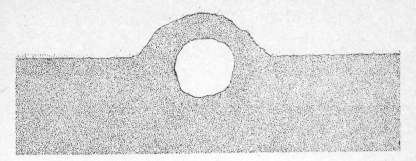

FIG. 13 Surface mole run.

enough for the mole to be able to push its body into the ground, simply displacing some of the soil upwards to make the surface ridge, while the rest is compacted into the side of the burrow. When more resistance is encountered, instead of the breast stroke action, the mole digs with one hand at a time. The action is illustrated in Fig. 14. The hind feet are used to brace the body against the sides of the tunnel, and one forelimb is also

FIG. 14 How the mole digs.

pressed firmly into the earth below the animal. In the figure the right fore foot (or hand) is being used as a brace. At the same time, the left "hand" thrusts sideways and upwards with a digging or shovelling motion. This may be repeated more than once, when the mole rotates its body through nearly 180 degrees, and starts digging with the left and bracing with the right hand.

Surface runs are mainly made during the warmer months, when the soil fauna is active in the upper layers of the soil. Some surface runs represent explorations of an area, and the mole may only pass along them once. Others are repeatedly visited and are used as feeding grounds when sufficient worms and insects are present in them, but none is as permanent as the deep burrows which are associated with molehills.

These deep burrows are constructed using the same single-handed technique just described. However, when the mole is working at a depth where a raised roof cannot be pushed above the surface, a considerable amount of loose soil is produced. This is thrown back along the tunnel; the hind feet assist in the process. The mole may dig several feet of burrow, or it may only excavate underground for a shorter distance, when it proceeds to expel the soil to the surface. It turns around and pushes the soil back along the burrow, using one fore limb "like the blade of a bulldozer," as this action is so graphically described by Gillian Godfrey. The other three limbs are used to move the animal itself. When a mole is starting an underground tunnel system, the first lot of spoil – the first molehill – appears at the site where the ground was first entered. Farther along the burrow, vertical shafts are constructed at irregular intervals, and the soil is pushed up the shaft immediately behind the area of current excavation.

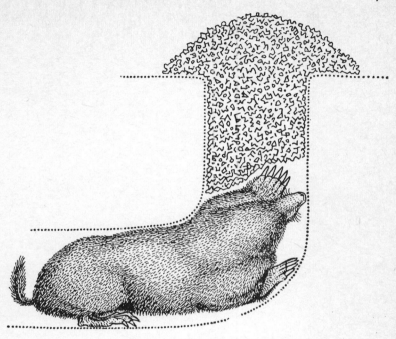

FIG. 15 How a molehill is made.

The process of making a molehill is interesting and demonstrates the surprising strength of the animal. Some older accounts wrongly suggest that the soil is pushed up with the head and shoulders. In fact, the action is similar to that used in digging, but the mole pushes directly with one front foot at the soil (Fig. 15) as it enters the bottom of the vertical shaft. Where the tunnel is near the surface, this will not be such a strenuous task, but to push the spoil up from burrows as much as one and a half feet (half a metre) below the surface must be a herculean labour. S. Skoczen, who has made the most thorough investigations of the process of burrowing, has shown that as much as

10 lbs (6 kg) of soil may be evacuated in twenty minutes. This is about fifty times the weight of the mole itself and corresponds to a 12-stone miner moving 4 tons in twenty minutes, or 12 tons an hour. It should be remembered that the mole has both to dig the soil and to push it up out of its "mine," with no mechanical aids. In our highly-mechanised coal mines, the output per worker at the coal face is only about 1 ton per hour.

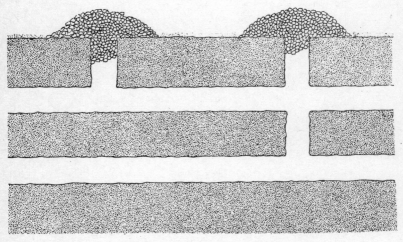

FIG. 16 The burrow system of the mole.

Moles construct quite complicated burrow systems (Fig. 16). Tunnels may be excavated at different levels, and these may be used at different times of year. In the centuries-old pasture known as Park Grass at Rothamsted Experimental Station, a similar pattern of molehills could be observed year after year. In particular, one long row of molehills running parallel to a track appeared annually, usually in January. It seemed that about that time the moles moved into their "winter quarters," that is to say, they opened up the deep burrows which had become partially blocked by falling earth, probably disturbed by the heavy tread of animals moving overhead. The same vertical shafts were used each time, probably after they had also been freed from loose soil. Last year's molehills had, of course, been removed or spread on the surface during the previous summer.

The probable reason for moles moving into burrows at different depths at different times of year is that in summer the food may be captured near the surface, while when the weather gets colder it can only be found in deeper, warmer soil. We know that worms retreat deeper into the ground in winter and that some insects do likewise. Others remain near to the surface, but they are immobilised by the cold and so are not easily available to the moles.

Molehills appear above snow, and on the surface of ground that has frozen hard like concrete. This has sometimes been interpreted to suggest that the animals are able to dig through this hard-frozen earth. Of course, they are digging in the soft warm soil below the frozen zone and are expelling the spoil through pre-existing vertical shafts. Crops of new molehills often appear just when the weather gets colder. These are, as already suggested, sometimes caused as a result of repairing old burrows, but they may equally be from the excavation of entirely new ones.

From the process of producing molehills, it is clear that these animals can turn round in burrows which are only slightly greater in diameter than the girth of the moles themselves.

As well as shallow runs and deep burrows, open trenches are also produced. As already mentioned, these have been described as rutting runs or "traces d'amour," though they are probably not in any way connected with the sex life of the animals. I think that they are often simply carelessly constructed surface tunnels in sandy soil and that the roof of the burrow has collapsed. They have also been observed at the soil-snow interface. It should be remembered that snow keeps the soil warm, and that moles which have gone into deeper burrows during frosty weather when the surface of the ground is bare may move up into the superficial layers when a blanket of snow has fallen. There are even records of moles making tunnels in the snow itself though, as no food will be present in this medium, this activity is difficult to explain.

Several observers have said that male and female moles construct and inhabit different patterns of tunnels. The suggestion is that females build an irregular network, while males make one long, straight burrow with others branching off it. It is true that in the breeding season males may make straight burrows in their migrations in search of a mate, but normally there seems no set pattern in the habitation of either sex. As the same burrows may be occupied by males or females at different times, and as a burrow originally occupied by an individual of one sex may, on its removal, be taken over by one of the opposite sex, there is evidently no rigid separation of territories or restriction to any particular type of excavation. This topic is dealt with further in the discussion of territorial behaviour (p. 107).

It must be stressed that, particularly in clay soils in woodlands, a number of mole burrows exist for many years and are used by generation after generation of moles. Some of these individuals are fortunate enough to find an unoccupied burrow in their youth, and they may never need to do any more digging than to repair and maintain this system. This subject is dealt with in more detail in the sections on mole activity in different habitats.

Except in such cases a young mole starting its independent life in summer has to construct its own tunnel system. It may live entirely above ground at first, producing easily recognisable signs where it scrabbles about among grass and moss. Very superficial burrows may be made among the grass roots. The next stage is usually to make superficial tunnels. Animals may make numerous starts to such systems, then emerge and move over the surface to try somewhere else. The final stage is the start of a deep run with its corresponding molehills. When only a few yards of deep run have been dug, the mole spends much of its time in the superficial burrows and among the vegetation. It is not surprising that, during the time the animals are living above ground, they most often form the food of predatory birds.

Although most moles seen on the surface during the summer months are young individuals, born during that year, older moles do sometimes come out of their burrows. A very interesting instance was reported by P. Morris. During a very dry summer at Cap Gris Nez in north France, the ground was hard and dry. Several moles were captured in Longworth small mammal traps, and others were caught by hand tearing grass tussocks. No molehills or other signs of burrowing were observed during this period of drought. Although there is no published report of such a striking incident in Britain, we usually find an increased number of corpses above ground in very dry weather, and it seems likely that moles come above ground more often than is usually imagined.

The mole's nest, used for sleeping, is simply an enlarged section of the burrow, filled with dry grass or dead leaves. It is usually indistinguishable from above the ground, at least in clay soils. There is usually no opening to the surface in the proximity of the nest, so the soil excavated has had to be moved quite a distance along the burrows before being expelled, and the maker has had quite an excursion collecting the bedding. How this may be performed is described on p. 52. More than one nest has been found in the tunnel system used by one mole. The nest in which the young are born may be similar to that used for rest, though it is often rather larger.

The "fortress" has already been mentioned, as a large hill containing a nest. Many authors have described these structures as containing an elaborate network of tunnels, often arranged in a regular pattern. In my experience the fortress is a comparatively rare phenomenon. For some reason, instead of simply making a structureless spoil heap which is of no further interest to its builder, an occasional mole on a rare occasion produces a far larger aggregation of soil, a virtual mountain in comparison with the normal molehill. The animal then burrows into its mountain and makes a nest in it. These mole mountains are built by both males and females, though a high proportion are used by females when they give birth to their young in early spring. Whether or not the females take some fortresses over from the males which built them is not known. There is no evidence that the male mole, like the stickleback, builds a nest as a means of enticing a female and persuading her to accept his attentions!

There are indeed burrows in the larger fortresses, but these seem to be irregularly constructed. Caches of worms have also been located there. Fortresses have been said to be produced in greatest numbers in areas liable to flooding, and I have indeed seen more in Woodwalton Fen, where flooding is frequent, than in Monks Wood, where the ground is never submerged (though tunnels may fill with water during a wet season). However, we had two fortresses only a yard apart built in a grass field near our research station, in a situation that never flooded and where the drainage was good. Young were produced in a nest in one fortress, and when this was disturbed the mother moved them to the other. The place we have seen most fortresses is the Breck, with sandy, well-drained soil that is never flooded. Here the explanation may be that it is difficult to bury a nest in the thin soil. This suggestion is made more probable by the smaller size of these "fortresses" which are often not much bigger than the ordinary hill found on a clay soil, but containing a nest at the base. From these remarks, it is clear that the mole fortress is still a mysterious erection, and one needing much further study.

The construction of the amorphous molehill, and of the more complicated though rare mole fortress, is usually looked upon as the nearest this animal gets to "building." However, when repairing a deep burrow, the mole may show remarkable skill in erecting an earthen arch and in producing a vaulted structure of considerable complexity. It is well known that if a burrow is broken, it is rapidly repaired, and this action is used to indicate whether or not the tunnel is still occupied. Sometimes a breach in the roof of the burrow is simply plugged up with loose soil, and a new length of excavation is made avoiding this region and connecting the undamaged burrow on either side. Often, however, the hole is repaired by pushing up soil which is compacted into a new roof; this I would describe as real "building."

This process is usually seen to be used in mending quite small holes, and it does not seem to be very noteworthy. However, when a burrow has a considerable section removed, the

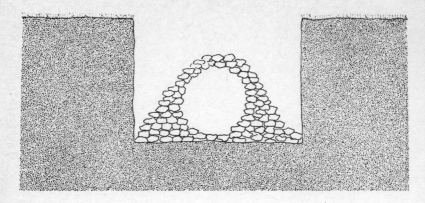

FIG. 17 Repairs to severe damage to a burrow.

potentialities of the mole in building are more fully demonstrated. I first saw this when a Friesian live trap had been
removed from a run. This left an oblong hole over a foot long
as an interruption to the run. The mole thereupon made its
repair not by burrowing underground, but by building a roof
as shown in Fig. 17. The animal scooped up lumps of clay the
size of a walnut, and stuck these together to form an arch. In
nature such severe damage to a run may not be common, but
the reactions of the animal do demonstrate how flexible is its
behaviour pattern and how unexpected are its responses. The
mole is certainly not a dim, helpless creature.

CHAPTER 7

TECHNIQUES OF STUDYING MOLES

Moles are often thought of as "mysterious" and difficult to observe and study. This chapter is intended to suggest how some of this mystery may be dispersed.

My first advice is to start by making a systematic study of mole workings in your area. You may be surprised by the result. For instance, most people have never realised that the soil in the woods they often visit is riddled with mole tunnels, though molehills are seldom seen. Molehills are the obvious sign that the animals are busy in pasture, but "crops" of new hills often appear at different times of year. It is interesting to find how much soil can be displaced in twenty-four hours. This is quite an easy task if the existing hills are levelled, so that new spoil thrown on to the surface can be recognised and, if required, weighed. If you can compare mole workings in different soil types and different habitats, and try to study the possible effects of the weather on activity, for instance of flooding or of frost (possibly, in a severe spell, measuring the distance down into the earth that is actually frozen), you will learn a great deal about mole behaviour.

Various methods are used to tell whether mole runs are occupied, or whether all the animals have been caught or driven away. Breaks are made in tunnels, and they are examined to see if they are repaired. The inside of a used tunnel has a characteristic, almost "polished" appearance, which is soon lost if no animals pass along. If vegetation, particularly grass, is growing above a fairly superficial tunnel, within two or three days of it being untenanted characteristic white plant roots appear and soon grow right across the cavity. When animals are running up and down they prevent these roots from developing.

Much can be learned by observations from the train, particularly when you look down on to fields from the top of an embankment. The whole pattern of the tunnel system can often be observed. You may, in spring, be able to see how the moles have invaded the crops from the hedgerow and ditches where their burrows have not been damaged by ploughing, harrowing and the other processes of cultivation.

After a time the study of "molesigns" may begin to pall, and you may wish to see more of the creatures themselves. In fact, particularly in early or mid-summer, you are likely to come across a live mole before long. Though even with experience it is impossible to guarantee that, on any one day, you will actually see, and be able to capture, a living mole, in the course of a few weeks you should certainly see several. These may be crossing a road, or scrabbling about among the grass or, more often, making superficial tunnels in grass or in recently-cultivated arable soil. These can then be caught quite easily by a sudden grab, though the captive will resist and may bite. The safest way to pick him up is by the tail, which is usually elevated in such a way as to make seizing it easy (Fig. 18). The late Albert Armsby, a most skilful mole-catcher, sometimes demonstrated an amusing trick. Having recognised the movement of a mole in a superficial tunnel, he jumped in the air and landed with one foot on either side of it, when the terrified creature surfaced at great speed! Particularly during a drought

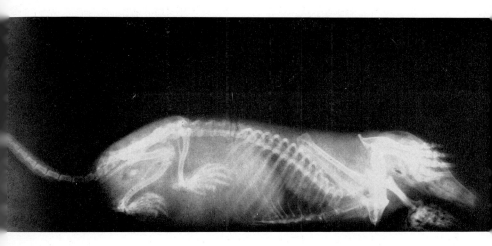

3. Radiographs of a live specimen of *Talpa europaea*, photographed in a cardboard cylinder. *Above*, from the side. *Below*, from above. Note the position of the fore limbs, pushed far forward beneath the neck; the large sternum; and the extent to which one hind limb has been abducted from the body, to place the foot against the side wall of the tunnel. Note also the large tibial sesamoid in the hind foot, giving the appearance of six toes.

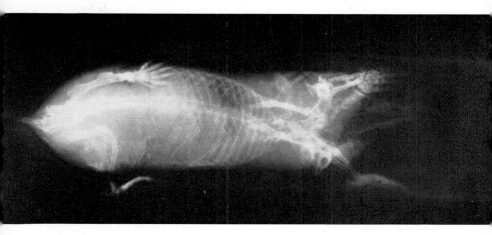

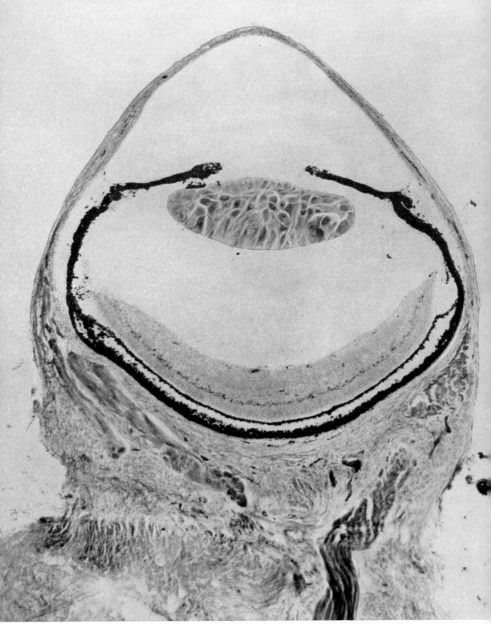

4. This horizontal section through the eye of the mole reveals a "conical" cornea, a deep anterior chamber, a minute but conventionally proportioned pupil, a cellular lens and a layered retina.

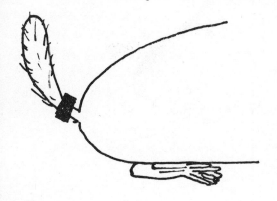

FIG. 18 Normal position of tail in living mole, showing also the method of ringing.

young moles may be unable to start a tunnel system and are often compelled to live above ground for some weeks.

It is more difficult to capture moles in deep burrows. You will often see soil erupting over the top of a molehill, like a small volcano in action. Attempts to dig the animal out are seldom successful, as it may be as much as a foot below the surface at the bottom of a vertical shaft, and before you have dug sufficiently it may have retreated a long way down its tunnel.

Many attempts have been made to devise an efficient live trap. Young animals are said to be caught when a bucket is sunk beneath the surface of a burrow, but many have failed totally with this technique. However, in 1636 Gervase Markham reported in his interesting publication, *Inrichment of the Weald of Kent*, that this method might have spectacular results. He writes:

"Take a live Moale in the moneth of March, which is their bucking or ingendring time, and put it into a deepe brasse Bason, or other deepe smooth Vessell, out of which the

Moale cannot creepe, and then at evening bury it in the earth up to the brimme, and so leave it, and the imprisoned Moale will presently beginne to strike, or complaine or call, so that all the Moales in the ground will come to it, and tumbling into the Vessell, they are prisoners also, and the more prisoners, the greater will bee the noise; and the more noise, the more Moales will come to the rescue, so that I have seene 50 or 60 taken in one night, and in one Vessell or brasse kettle."

I am afraid that I am somewhat sceptical about the accuracy of this statement.

The common scissor trap (p. 135) which normally kills may be adapted to prevent it closing completely. This may some-times catch moles alive, but if they are undamaged they often escape, and those remaining in the traps are often injured and die soon after. I fear that some which escape may also be hurt and die a lingering death. I do not recommend this method.

The most efficient device is the Friesian Tunnel trap, still manufactured in the Netherlands. Fig. 19 shows its construc-tion. A block of wood has a round hole about the diameter of a mole burrow bored through its length. Two "portcullis" doors close this by entering slots near each end of the tunnel.

FIG. 19 Working drawing of Friesian Live Trap. These drawings are intended to help those who wish to construct this trap. The base is usually made of a block of elm, though other soft woods will do. It is $12'' \times 4\frac{1}{2}'' \times 4\frac{1}{2}''$ (30 cm $\times$ 11 cm $\times$ 11 cm) bored along its length with a cylindrical hole $2\frac{1}{2}''$ (6.3 cm) in diameter. The "portcullis" doors which close the trap are made of $3/16''$ (5 mm) plywood, but it is better to use perspex sheet which is less liable to jam in the slot when the trap closes to catch a mole. A, side view; B, end view; C, oblique isometric.

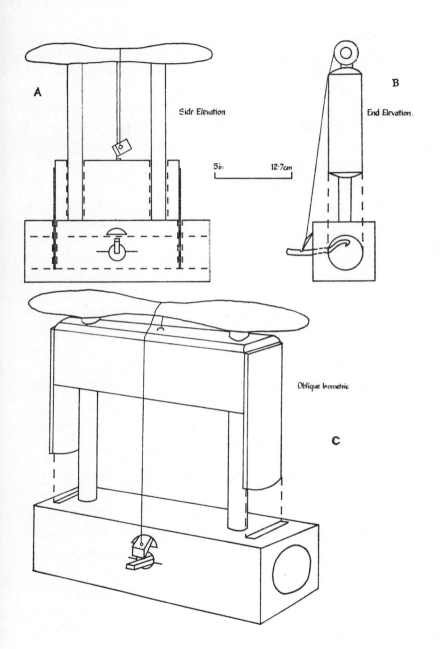

A

Side Elevation

B

End Elevation.

5in   12·7cm

Oblique Isometric

C

A trigger in the middle of the tunnel releases this portcullis when a mole is trying to pass through. The trap is not easy to set. A suitable straight mole run must be found, and a length, the size of the trap, removed. Then the holes at each end of the trap must be placed carefully to coincide with the openings of the burrow. In clay soils, the best results are obtained by moulding the soils to make a good junction. The disadvantages of this trap are first that, even when great care is taken in setting it, in about 50 per cent of cases the mole does not enter, but bungs it up with soil and digs a new tunnel around it, and secondly that unless it is examined frequently, say at least every eight hours, moles may die inside from cold, wet, starvation and from battering themselves against the wooden walls. It is often advantageous to put this trap in a run and wedge it open, so moles get used to running through, before setting it to capture them.

A. J. B. Rudge produced a useful improvement. He cut a hole in the side of the trap and fitted a tin which was filled with hay and also contained some food, usually worms. Moles usually survived up to twenty-four hours in this. However, if you are interested in territorial behaviour, this may be too long a period, as it is possible that when a mole is in the trap, its "territory" could be invaded by an intruder. This point is discussed in Chapter 9.

Animal populations, particularly those of mice and voles, are often studied by obtaining data by marking captured individuals which are then released. Subsequent trapping includes recaptures of these, and also individuals not previously caught. Thus if 100 marked individuals are released into an area and then subsequently 500 trapped individuals include ten of those which have been marked, the total population of the area may be assumed to be in the region of 5,000. When trapping continues over a period, allowances must be made for death, migration and birth, and sophisticated mathematical formulae are employed to estimate the population more accurately. Unfortunately this technique does not seem applicable to moles. Too small numbers are usually captured for marking, and the behaviour of those released, which may remain in one area, and of the unmarked individuals, whose distribution may not overlap, at least in pasture, may prevent meaningful calculations from being made.

Nevertheless, it is useful to mark individuals so they can be recognised again. This can be most easily accomplished by clipping small patches of fur. It takes several weeks for this to grow again and obliterate the mark. By one or two clips in different areas, dozens of individuals could be temporarily distinguished.

A more permanent mark is obtained by using a numbered metal ring. This technique has often been used with rodents, when a ring on the leg does not apparently do any harm or noticeably affect the animals' behaviour. In the mole a ring, made from a strip of monel metal 15 × 3 mm, weighing 200 mg, is most conveniently fitted round the base of the club-like tail (Fig. 18). The results of studies of marked moles are given in Chapter 9. Incidentally, although ringing should only be done by competent workers, taking care not to harm the animals, yet there is no legal control of such practices, where wild mammals are concerned. In contrast, bird-ringing is now strictly controlled. Permits must be obtained from the Nature Conservancy, and are only given to suitable persons, usually with the approval of the British Trust for Ornithology. It is perhaps a pity that mammals do not receive the same protection. However, a ring weighing 200 mg, worn by a 100 gm mole, is approximately equivalent only to the burden of a large wrist-watch (weighing $2\frac{1}{2}$ oz) worn by man, so it need not be a major inconvenience, though if too tight necrosis of the base of the tail may occur. Such a ring, worn by a half-ounce (15 gm) mouse may be a more severe burden, as it is equivalent to a two-pound weight affixed to a human being.

Gillian Godfrey developed a most ingenious technique for studying animal movements using radioactive rings, and when this was applied to moles very interesting results were obtained. In essence, a radioactive source consisting of 80–100 microcuries of Cobalt 60, enclosed in a metal capsule, was soldered to an ordinary tail ring of the type described above. It must be stressed that this is not a technique which can be used by an amateur, or by anyone except under most rigorously controlled conditions. To avoid possible damage to the experimenter or to others from uncontrolled radiation, rings have to be stored in thick lead containers and have to be handled with tongs behind ramparts of lead bricks. Precautions have also to be taken to make sure that the moles do not escape from the area studied and distribute the radioactive rings around the country. This technique has also been used by A. J. B. Rudge and by J. Haeck, who substituted radioactive silver (Ag 110) for Gillian Godfrey's Cobalt 60 source.

The marked mole is detected using a portable Geiger counter, mounted on a light pole. The Geiger counter is connected to headphones, in which the frequency of the "clicks" indicates the proximity of the mole. The animal does not seem to be disturbed by vibration caused by the footfalls of the observer, if he avoids stepping immediately above its position. The ring (and so the animal to which it is attached) can be detected up to one foot (30 cm) underground. The disadvantage of this method is that only one animal in an area can be followed with certainty. There is also some evidence that long exposure to this level of radiation may damage the mole.

The main results obtained with radioactive rings were of the periodic activity of the mole in the wild. Fig. 20 is derived from

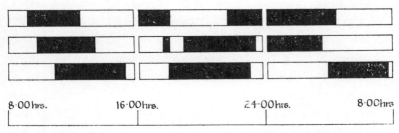

8·00 hrs.   16·00hrs.   24·00hrs.   8·00hrs

FIG. 20 Periodicity of activity of a mole in the field. After G. Godfrey. Black=rest, white=active, either walking or digging.

Gillian Godfrey's studies and shows the three periods of rest, and the three of activity, each twenty-four hours. This technique has also proved invaluable in showing the range of movement of moles in pasture (p. 102). Work with a radioactive ring has been combined in studies of a larger number of animals marked with ordinary, numbered rings.

Mole populations may also be studied with ordinary traps of the type used to control them, for instance, the Scissor or the Duffus (p. 135). If an area is trapped out, this clearly gives an accurate measure of the population, but has the disadvantage that this population, having been destroyed, cannot be studied further. However, recolonisation of the area can then be investigated. A great deal of information can, in fact, be derived from this type of trapping, particularly when it is used in different habitats.

I have already discussed the problem of catching live moles. Having caught an animal, the next problem is how to keep it alive. A newly caught mole is probably starving; it may have been active for some hours and it is in a strange environment. The essential first step is to persuade it to feed. Although captive moles may be maintained on many articles of food, including liver, baby mice, mealworms and maggots, they always seem to prefer live earthworms, particularly large *Lumbricus terrestris*. Newly caught moles often refuse any other type of food; if they are offered some three large worms (a large *L. terrestris* weighs about 5 gm) they will probably consume these in a matter of minutes. They will then explore their surroundings and if a small box containing hay is present they will crawl in and go to sleep. They will probably sleep for at least four hours, possibly for up to seven hours, and when they awake they will be, to all intents and purposes, domesticated and suitable subjects for further study.

Moles have been kept successfully in various types of container. At one conference where several scientists combined their experiences, "ammunition boxes" were repeatedly mentioned as suitable. These are strong, army-surplus wooden boxes about 3 feet long by 18 inches wide and 18 inches deep (1 m × 50 cm × 50 cm), and they were generally half-filled with soil. Personally I think that it may be best not to include so much soil, for if this is not compact, and does not have well-defined burrows, the moles may have difficulties in discovering their food. I used a wooden box, 60 × 35 cm and 25 cm deep, with a wooden lid fixed over half the top, and a movable glass plate – to allow the animal to be watched – covering the rest. In the bottom I put "bulb fibre," about 2 cm deep. This contained some charcoal, which absorbs excretory products without quickly becoming foul. A small box, 15 × 11 × 10 cm, with an entry hole, fixed at one end of the larger box and filled with hay, served as a nest. I have kept moles for many weeks in this way. Sometimes an apparently healthy animal died, but more often its captivity ended because it escaped by pushing off the lid.

Some workers have used far more complicated structures. S. Skoczen introduced a method which has been adapted by A. J. B. Rudge and which has allowed moles to be kept in good health for up to eight months. Long artificial tunnels are made by sewing together zinc-coated woven wire, and this was used to produce a complex run system. These tunnels were attached to a nest box. The moles spent most of their active periods in these simulated mole runs. They did not appear to suffer from the absence of earth, which in any case was apt to get foul in a few days. Electric contacts and time-measuring devices can be attached to the tunnels, to record mole activity and behaviour.

I adapted the simple box method to study the mole's behaviour and to serve as a type of "aktograph," which recorded any periodicity in activity. I first balanced the box in such a way that, when the mole came out of its nest, the box tipped over and made an electric contact and rang a bell. The bell could be placed far enough away to avoid disturbing the mole, but in a position where it alerted the observer. This arrangement made it possible for me to observe the mole's activity over several days, and to share with the animal its periods of rest. I found the process informative, it enabled me to determine, for instance, how much food could be consumed, but other members of my household were less enthusiastic about the

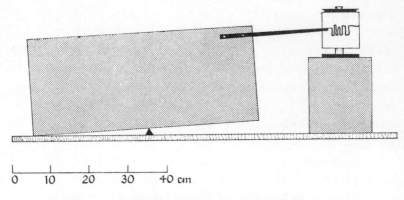

FIG. 2I "Aktograph" to study mole behaviour.

irregular nocturnal disturbances caused whenever the bell was rung, and the experiment and the observer were temporarily banished to an outhouse.

As a longer term study, it was obviously desirable to record the mole's movements automatically. This was done by fitting a pen which traced the movements on a paper on a revolving drum (Figs. 21 and 22). The pen was of the type used with a thermograph, using the slow-drying ink supplied for such an apparatus. The revolving drum, which contained a clockwork motor, and which completed one revolution in twenty-four

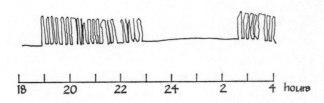

FIG. 22 Tracing from drum showing mole activity.

hours, had also been supplied with a thermograph, but could have been simply constructed by attaching a suitable tin to an inexpensive clock. The records confirmed that the mole usually had three periods of sleep, and three of activity, every twenty-four hours. In fact, the results proved to be strikingly similar to those obtained by Gillian Godfrey when she studied the periodic activity of wild moles in the field. We both found that the hours of movement and of rest were not entirely regular, and we obtained no confirmation of the statement by countrymen that trapping is likely to be most successful at certain and precise times of day. As mentioned above, moles exhibited very similar patterns of behaviour when supplied with unlimited food or when starved for periods of up to twenty-four hours.

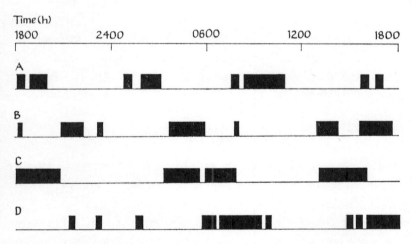

FIG. 23 Behaviour of moles under different feeding regimes. The black rectangles indicate activity, the base lines show when the animals were asleep. A, unlimited earthworms; B and C, starved; D, unlimited liver.

CHAPTER 8

LIFE IN DIFFERENT HABITATS

I HAVE already said that the mole is found in a wider range of habitats than almost any other British mammal. Its mode of life is different under these different conditions. It is affected particularly by the nature of the soil, which may be hard and intractable like clay, or easily worked, like sand or peat. The food supply is also important, and this varies from 1–2 tons, mainly of earthworms, to an acre ($2\frac{1}{2}$–5 metric tonnes to a hectare) in deciduous woodland and rich pasture, down to a fiftieth of this amount in the sandy soils of Breckland in Suffolk. The commonly-held view that moles can only exist where there is a plentiful food supply is clearly erroneous. In this chapter, I deal with the mode of life in a number of different and distinct habitats.

DECIDUOUS WOODLAND ON CLAY SOIL

This section is based mainly on my findings in Monks Wood National Nature Reserve. This has an area of 387 acres (150 ha) of deciduous woodland, of the type which, 2,000 years ago, covered most of the clay soils of southern Britain. The main trees are oak and ash, with hazel and many other species as a shrub layer, and with dog's mercury, primroses and bluebells among the most prominent herbaceous plants. The wood is not "virgin" forest, though most of the area has been under tree cover for hundreds, and probably thousands, of years. There has been an active management policy for the period covered by historical records. There were considerable areas of "coppice with standards." The coppice, mainly hazel, was cut about every ten years to produce stakes, handles and pea-sticks, while the standards, mainly oaks, were cut on a much longer rotation. This system continued until 1914, though since the middle of the nineteenth century game preservation was important. In 1919 much of the more valuable timber was felled, and many of the present trees have grown up from the stumps. To-day the wood is being managed by the Nature Conservancy. Some areas are being coppiced, some will, it is hoped, revert to high forest. Some twenty miles of rides are cut annually; their margins provide a valuable degree of diversity, and their trodden turf makes the detection of moles easy.

Monks Wood contains most of the mammals associated with woodland. These include wood mice, field voles, shrews, hedge-hogs, weasels, stoats, rabbits and hares. Red squirrels have been replaced by grey, badgers died out some years ago, and only occasional individuals now pass through. A red deer suddenly appeared and stayed for six months in 1966, and muntjac often enter and stay for varying periods. When I first visited the wood, I was told that moles occurred but were uncommon. As will appear, they are in fact present in quite good numbers. As far as I can tell, the moles have never before been trapped within the wood, though it is possible that some trapping may have been done, from time to time, in the surrounding fields. The wood was then, no doubt, a focus for reinfestation.

The invertebrate fauna is rich, and worms alone amount to nearly 7 oz to the square yard (220 gm to the square metre), which is equivalent to 1 ton to the acre ($2\frac{1}{4}$ tonnes to the hectare). The greatest weight of worms is made up of *Lumbricus terrestris*. The next most important species of probable value to the mole is *Lumbricus rubellus*.

The most noteworthy fact regarding the wood, as a mole habitat, is the paucity of "molesigns." This obviously accounts for the idea that the animals were rare. With careful examination, however, one realises that burrows are very numerous even if few molehills appear. The whole of the wood appears to contain an anastomosing network of permanent tunnels. I have no evidence as to how long a time a burrow continues in use, except that some which existed ten years ago look much the same to-day. They must have been used, in that period, by at least three generations of moles.

By trapping out various areas, we have obtained estimates of the population. This would appear to be between 400, in winter, and 900, in summer, when the young have left their mother. These estimates are, of course, only approximate, but they give some idea of the degree of magnitude of the population. Thus there seems to be between $1\frac{1}{2}$ and $2\frac{1}{2}$ moles to the acre (3–6 to the hectare).

Molehills are not entirely absent. They appear sporadically but seldom in large numbers. They consist mainly of the black humus-rich topsoil, but often in the middle of the heap quite an amount of the yellowish clay is visible. This suggests that while this was being dug, the tunnel was being deepened. I have tried to correlate the appearance of the hills with changes in the weather. They certainly appear during cold spells, suggesting that deeper tunnels are being brought back into use. I have seldom seen enough soil on the surface to suggest that a whole new burrow system is being excavated.

In very wet weather, although Monks Wood is never submerged, yet many burrows contain some water. These may be abandoned temporarily, though by no means inevitably, and it is surprising how clean and free from mud the fur of a live mole stays. A dead one, dropped on to a wet enough surface, is at once plastered with mud.

When we have a dry summer, the clay soil cracks widely. Extra big cracks may coincide with mole burrows. These may be repaired with the damper soil from deep down, or they too may be temporarily evacuated.

In summer, many signs of surface activity by young moles can be distinguished. Tunnels are made among moss and grass on the rides. There is very little evidence of these young animals constructing deep burrows *de novo*.

Elsewhere (Chapter 9) I consider data from trapping in Monks Wood more thoroughly, when discussing the problem of territorial behaviour. For the present I only need report that moles appear to move more widely than they do in pasture, and that an animal removed a distance of several hundred yards found its way back to its original station in a few hours.

Mole numbers have appeared to remain relatively stable for several years. The surplus young are evidently either eaten by predators or they migrate into the surrounding fields. The fortunate mole which, in its youth, finds a stretch of burrow which it can occupy lives for the rest of its existence a life of ease and luxury. It seldom needs to do anything so strenuous as digging, and its food must usually be very easily obtained. Except for fights with its own species, and perhaps encounters with weasels, which are not infrequently caught in mole traps, life must be rather boring.

All other deciduous woodlands I have examined in Britain and on the Continent of Europe seem to harbour moles, except sometimes those with thin, stony soils on mountain sides. In the hilly wooded slopes of the valleys in Luxemburg, for instance, moles are widespread, and seem to live very much like those in Monks Wood.

CONIFEROUS FOREST

It is commonly said that, in coniferous woods, there is insufficient food to support moles. This may well be true in some instances, though how many I cannot say as I have examined insufficient sites. However, it is not true of the Tentsmuir Forest in Fife in Scotland. This is an old pine forest, where these trees have existed for centuries. The moles there behave in a manner not unlike those in Monks Wood. Though the soil is more sandy, it is rich in vegetable matter below the trees, and permanent burrows abound. I have not had the opportunity of studying the soil fauna scientifically, but from a brief examination I should think it poorer than Monks Wood but richer than the Breck. J. Oppermann studied moles in several pine forests near Berlin in Germany. These seemed to flourish, but a high proportion of their food was insect material, particularly cockchafer grubs and Cerambycid larvae. These moles were smaller than those from other habitats, but this may not be related to a sparse diet. It would be interesting to study many other coniferous woods, particularly where spruce has been planted to replace deciduous trees, to see how the soil fauna, including the mole, has been affected.

FENLAND

The second habitat where I have studied the mole extensively is Woodwalton Fen in Huntingdonshire. This comprises 514

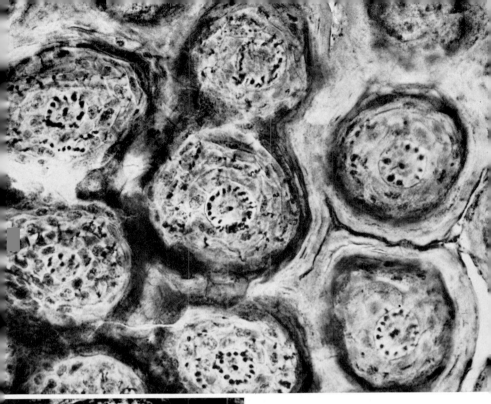

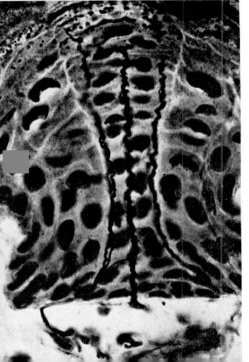

5. *Above*, horizontal section through the tip of the snout of the mole. Seven complete Eimer's organs are shown. Each has an outer ring of epithelial cells containing few nerve terminals and an inner circle of epithelial cells with a single axial vertical nerve terminal with a series of surrounding satellite terminals. *Below*, vertical section through one Eimer's organ. The axial nerve terminal passes through the centre rod of epithelial cells.

6. *Above*, close up of snout of mole emerging from a tube, showing vibrissae encircling the muzzle. *Below*, horizontal section of dermal root of a vibrissa from mole's muzzle. The central hair is surrounded by a vertical plexus of nerve terminals.

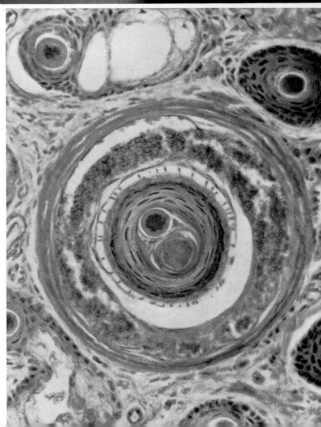

acres (208 ha) of undrained fen. Prior to the draining of Whittlesea Mere in 1851, much of the county was fen. It then became arable farmland, but this area was preserved by the Hon. N. C. Rothschild as a nature reserve. He bequeathed it to the Society for the Promotion of Nature Reserves, who now lease it (at a nominal rent) to the Nature Conservancy, who are responsible for its management. Parts of the fen were cut for fuel (peat) in the nineteenth century, and much has been over-grown with scrub, encouraged by a fall in the water table, a process now being actively reversed. Grass rides are maintained by mowing, and mole activities are most easily observed in them, though, in fact, most parts of the reserve have some signs when carefully examined, and when the observer can make his way through the areas of dense scrub. The fen is frequently flooded, being mostly covered by two or three feet ($\frac{2}{3}$–1 metre) of water, on several occasions in most years. Floods usually occur in winter, but occasionally they happen in summer. In 1968 the fen was under water for some weeks after phenomenal rain on 10th July.

The soil fauna is sparse as compared with Monks Wood. Few worms are encountered when digging, and few emerge when the soil is treated with formalin as recommended by F. Raw. However, during the summer floods of 1968 we realised that worms were slightly more plentiful than we had imagined, though *Lumbricus terrestris* seems to be very uncommon and absent from most areas. Although worms are not harmed by the cold floods in winter, in warm weather when their metabol-ism is increased and the oxygen content of the water decreases, they may be drowned. After some days of flooding, specimens of *Octolasium lacteum* and *Lumbricus rubellus* were found dead on the surface of the flooded ground, but only in sufficient quantities to represent a food mass of less than a quarter the amount in Monks Wood. Insect larvae are quite abundant, including aggregations of large Tipulid larvae.

The main difference from Monks Wood is that new molehills appear on almost every day of the year. The soil is very easy to work, and I believe that the moles must constantly enlarge their underground feeding area to obtain sufficient food. Were the food as sparse as at Woodwalton Fen and the soil as intractable as in Monks Wood, I do not believe that moles could exist. When a flood occurs, the burrows are filled with water, and the moles swim to safety or are drowned. The animals do *not* survive by breathing pockets of air trapped in the soil. Moles are known to be excellent swimmers, and in fact the front feet are as well adapted for this purpose as for digging. I have heard that houses near Wageningen in the Netherlands may be invaded by numbers of moles driven out of riverside meadows when these are flooded. We have no precise knowledge of where our moles swim to, but they probably find refuge in the high earth banks surrounding the reserve. The interesting point is that, when the water retreats, they return so quickly, as sometimes new molehills are seen within two days of the water retreating from the same area. We do not know whether the same animals come back to their original sites, or whether their return is a more random process. We also have no idea how they "know" that the soil is dry enough to accommodate them. I was fortunate enough to witness the return of one mole after a period of flooding. This occurred about noon on 2nd January, 1966, and I made the following notes at the time.

"At about 12.10 p.m., on the ride at the south side of compartment 105, I saw a mole swimming into the cutting across the path made to let the water in from the channel between 105 and 106. The mole looked as if it were swimming purposefully, and when it reached the bank (which had been cut away with a spade where it landed) it scrambled quickly up the bank and just below the top it went straight into an open burrow. Again it looked as if it were purposefully homing into a familiar burrow. I heard it squeak soon after it had disappeared – it seemed to have gone about a yard in a few seconds."

I do not believe that the mole was actually homing. I wondered at the time if the squeaking meant that another mole had been encountered, but it was not prolonged as in a real fight, and no animal came to the surface, so if the swimmer did find the burrow inhabited, one of the animals went off, perhaps down a side tunnel, without much resistance.

BRECK

The Suffolk Breckland consists of poor sandy soil. In recent years much of it has been planted, mainly with conifers, by the Forestry Commission. Most of the area was previously rather poor grazing, but, where trees have not been planted, large areas have been ploughed and turned into arable. There is still some grass, some of which has been invaded by scrub, and part of the Breck is covered with heather.

The soil fauna is sparse. There are comparatively few earthworms, the commonest species being *Lumbricus rubellus* and *Allolobophora chloratica*. Insects and other arthropods are numerous, but the total weight of all these animals amount only to about 25 lb per acre (25 kg per hectare), which is only about a fiftieth of the weight of animals in the same area in Monks Wood.

In parts of the Breck, the sandy soil is only a few inches deep over a substratum of chalk. Here, in summer, the ground may be covered with a network of surface burrows, like an immense area of giant varicose veins. Each mole ranges over several acres, and many burrows are apparently only visited at intervals of several days. In deeper soils, deep burrows punctuated with molehills are found; here also parts of the system may be visited fairly infrequently. The immense amount of surface activity gives the erroneous impression that moles abound, but they actually exist in small numbers, as is shown by the difficulty experienced in trapping. Many traps, set over a period of days, may only catch one or two moles where a similar distribution in pasture in richer soil might catch two dozen.

Notwithstanding their rarity, worms form a significant part of the diet, but insects are consumed in large amounts. My colleague, J. P. Dempster, considers that a substantial number of Cinnabar moth pupae may be eaten, with a considerable effect on the number which survive the winter and emerge as moths the next summer. He also found that ant cocoons were eaten frequently, and one stomach of a female trapped in July contained no less than 932 cocoons of the ant *Lasius flavus*! The Breck mole evidently has a hard life, having to dig for a substantial part of its working hours.

The chalk grasslands of England really deserve a special section, but mole activity here is essentially similar to the Breck. Worms are comparatively rare, arthropods are common. Moles have a rather patchy distribution, but where they occur, the surface activity seems very great compared with their rather low numbers.

FARMLAND

Most of Britain is farmed in some way or other. Farmland provides a great variety of changing habitats. Farms are on all types of soil, and this profoundly affects the ecology of the area. For our purposes the main divisions are into grassland and arable, as the processes of cultivation greatly affect moles, but differences in the life pattern can be produced by many other factors.

Most workers have studied the mole on farmland, particularly on pasture during the winter. There have been fewer investigations on arable. However, the main efforts of mole-catchers have been on these arable fields, so a good deal of information is available. For some reason there is a tradition that moles should only be caught between 1st November and the end of June. Presumably from July to October the runs are difficult to see, and the crops would be damaged when the traps were set and inspected, but there is no difficulty in trapping during this "off season."

Grassland, particularly old grassland on good soil, has a rich soil fauna. Earthworms of many species abound, surface casts (producing Charles Darwin's "vegetable mould," the stone-free fertile upper layer) are made mainly by two species, *Allolobophora nocturna* and *Allolobophora longa*. Unfortunately these species do not like the plough, and reseeded leys contain few, and the population takes many years to recover. *Lumbricus terrestris* does not seem to be harmed by ploughing and digging, and it flourishes particularly when organic manures are used. Poor soils, like the Breck which we have just described, have, of course, a relatively poor fauna.

Conditions in permanent grass are not unlike those in deciduous woodland, except that there is more disturbance of the soil. Molehills are obviously prominent, but they are not made equally frequently at all times of year. In clay we find the same long-lasting permanent burrows, but in more friable soils the burrows are more transient. The work of Gillian Godfrey and others has shown that moles in grassland occupy particular areas, often covering some 450 sq. yards (about 400 sq. metres). The burrows are situated within this area; of course, even here there are many islands of untouched turf. The question of territorial behaviour is examined in Chapter 9, but although this is a complicated subject, there are some points which must be mentioned here. The highest density of moles measured by trapping, in England, is 18 to the acre (45 to the hectare). However, this was probably an overestimate, as some animals probably invaded the trapped area after others had been removed. About 4 moles to the acre (10 to the hectare) would seem to be as high a density as we often develop in those parts of our grassland which harbour moles. The interesting thing is the patchiness of this distribution. A large and apparently uniform field, all of it with a soil and fauna which might be expected to contain a high density of moles, may show signs of activity in only restricted areas. These may expand or contract in different years, but uniform infestation is rare. Why so many apparently suitable areas remain free, while moles struggle so hard to maintain themselves in more difficult habitats with a paucity of food, is a mystery.

When grass is ploughed, the tunnels are usually destroyed. Few moles are actually killed during ploughing, and the majority move temporarily into the hedgerows and ditch banks. When cultivation is completed, and the crop sown, reinvasion takes place. This may be quite rapid, with many yards, particularly of surface run, being constructed in a day. It is often possible to see the whole invasion pattern clearly in a corn crop, when the small plants above the burrows wilt because of damage to their roots. With the removal of hedgerows and the production of large, prairie-like fields, none of which is put down to grass, the mole may be exterminated over a wide area. In the fens the hedges have generally gone, but drainage ditches and their banks serve as refuges, and mole numbers seem to be maintained. In some cases harrowing and rolling may not damage the deeper runs, and moles may be left in the middle of fields after such shallow cultivations. This accounts for the appearance of isolated patches of molehills in the middle of a field. "Chemical Ploughing," in which grass and weeds are killed with the herbicide paraquat, a substance usually immediately immobilised by contact with the soil, may do little harm to moles – we know that earthworms survive this treatment better than mechanical ploughing. So some modern methods may not be harmful. However, if most modern trends in farming in Britain continue, I think that the mole will have a very thin time in many areas.

THE UPLANDS

Mole activity has been reported at nearly 3,000 feet (900 metres) in Britain, and at 6,000 feet (1,800 metres) in the alps. The upland area of which I have most experience in this connection is in Upper Teesdale, near the site of the new Cow Green Reservoir, at a height of 1,650 feet (500 metres) above sea-level. "Molesigns" are very apparent on many of the areas of loamy soil, so much so that about half of some areas must be covered with molehills. There are no molehills in surrounding

areas of acid peat, which indicates that there is a lower limit
to the quantity of food which is sufficient for these animals.
The peat has a very sparse fauna indeed. However, even the
loam is not very rich in invertebrates, probably the total mass
being under 100 lb per acre (100 kg per hectare), which is much
less than in lowland grassland. It is noticeable that mole
activity also follows roads which have been made up with limestone chippings even when these roads run over the peat. The
limestone has presumably affected the soil, making the conditions more suitable for invasion by earthworms.

There are very few moles causing this havoc to this upland
grass. In one isolated patch of loamy soil almost covered with
"molesigns," I only caught one mole, and examination of the
burrows indicated that it was the only inhabitant. In a lowland
clay soil half a dozen moles would have made less mess. Incidentally, examination of the stomach contents of this mole
showed that it had managed to collect a reasonable meal of
earthworms as a result of its strenuous activities. The same
amount of food, shared between two, might have been in-
adequate. This same area has also been investigated by A. W.
Davison and T. J. Bines, and their findings on the effects of
moles on the plant communities are discussed in Chapter 10.

The Welsh mountains have also been included in mole
surveys. In Snowdonia, C. Milner and D. F. Ball found that
moles were widespread, living up to 1,700 feet (500 metres) in
the more freely drained soils with a pH greater than 4, unless
such soils were so stony as to prevent their burrowing. They
were not present in the very acid soils; these, of course, had the
most depleted invertebrate fauna. As a rule the moles occupied
the areas most grazed by sheep, and so most enriched by sheep
dung, which in turn encouraged the development of earth-

worms. Also in Wales, P. Hope Jones showed that, in Merioneth, moles occur very widely. They are absent from the mobile dunes near the sea, but appear when these merge with stable grassland. They were not common above 1,000 feet (300 metres), but this was probably because the soil was unsuitable. Isolated colonies were found in suitable soil patches above this level; it is difficult to understand how the animals reached such places. They must have travelled quite a long and rocky road. The same thing was also noted by P. Hope Jones in other parts of Wales. He described an isolated mole colony at 2,700 feet (800 metres) on Cader Idris.

GARDENS

The first introduction many people have to the mole is the appearance of a row of piles of earth on their lawn. The damage is so great that they imagine they have been invaded by hundreds of the animals. In a small garden of, say, $\frac{1}{4}$ an acre, it is unlikely that there is more than one mole, though if he is caught, and there are woods or open fields nearby, he may easily be replaced.

Moles are clearly very destructive to lawns, and may damage growing plants, but the process is not cumulative. The first few days, while a tunnel system is being constructed, are the worst. If the soil is rich in earthworms, a large enough system of runs to collect food will soon be constructed, and then the production of molehills will, at least temporarily, cease. Sometimes even more damage is done by making networks of superficial tunnels in the grass, but this again is only a seasonal phenomenon.

I have been strongly attacked by many keen gardeners for

suggesting that they should learn to live with their moles! In sandy soils this may be impossible, for damage goes on all the year, but in clay a settled population is often there without the householder knowing. He thinks that, when the production of hills ceased, the animals have left. They may make a further set, but a smaller one, during cold weather, but otherwise they may give no evidence of their presence for months on end unless their runs are destroyed. If they *are* destroyed, the garden is left open to further invasion, and if the invaders do not find the existing burrows (which may fall in if not in constant use) they cause far more damage than would have occurred from the continuing presence of the existing population. It is true that your moles (or, more probably, mole, if your garden is small) may breed, and the young may cause damage as they establish themselves, but they are likely to migrate some distance, and if they escape the attentions of owls, dogs, cats and other predators, the damage is unlikely to occur on your property.

CHAPTER 9

TERRITORIAL BEHAVIOUR

MOLES hate their own species! If two are confined together in the same cage they will fight to the death. If a newly-killed mole is dropped into a box containing a live one, the reaction is sometimes startling. Had a worm or a piece of meat been so introduced, it would probably have been approached with some caution, and been dragged off to be eaten. But the dead mole may be attacked immediately with a frenzied outburst of what appears to the observer to be the most violent hatred. The corpse is lacerated and may be, cannabalistically, eaten. T. A. Quilliam reported several cases of moles escaping from their "ammunition boxes" (p. 88) and entering other boxes and killing the occupant. A. J. B. Rudge reported the forcing of metal barriers in his complex tunnel system (p. 89) by aggressive males who pursued and killed females.

Fighting has often been seen in the wild as well as in the laboratory. It appears to occur when one animal tries to invade another's territory, though it may be the result of a casual encounter. Sometimes a prolonged battle is reported, with one animal being killed. More often, after an exchange of blows, one of the animals considers that discretion is the better part of valour and retreats. Thus my colleague E. Pollard reported, "Movement was seen in disturbed bare ground on the east bank of the Alconbury brook among nettles and umbellifers on the edge of a cereal field. A mole emerged, ran about erratically, and returned below ground at the place of emergence. More disturbance was soon followed by the reappearance of a mole which ran off into nearby vegetation. A second mole came above ground, pursued the first momentarily, and then buried itself again." Similar encounters are described by Gillian Godfrey. As dead moles which are picked up in the field often show lesions which support the view that they have died in mortal combat with another member of their species, fights may be more often fatal than has been suggested. I suspect that a bite on the tip of the snout would soon cause death.

Some observers consider the male to be the most aggressive, and fights to be most frequent between "bucks," particularly during the breeding season. But the female appears to be as, or nearly as, aggressive. Fights can occur between males, between females, and between the sexes. "Social life" only seems to occur between mother and young for a brief period from birth to a few weeks after weaning, and for the unknown, but undoubtedly short, period during which copulation occurs.

There is no doubt that moles are aggressive, quarrelsome and solitary. The question to be decided is whether they actually live permanently in one place, one territory, which is in some way demarcated so that its existence can be recognised by an intruder, or whether their living conditions are more fluid. Much work has gone into investigating this problem.

This is not the place for a long discussion on territorial behaviour. Those interested should consult the authoritative book by V. C. Wynne-Edwards, *Animal Dispersion*, and the writings of W. H. Burt and of many other research scientists in various learned journals, or, if their interests are on a different level, the lively *Territorial Imperative* by Robert Ardrey. All that need be said here is that most mammals which are not nomadic are attached to certain areas. These have a *home range*, which is the area within which the animal moves about during its ordinary daily life. Then some, but by no means all, mammals have a *territory*, which they defend against other members of the same species, excepting, in most cases, members of their immediate family or of a social group. The territory may be the same area as the home range, or it may be a smaller zone around the nest. What we need to know is whether the mole has a home range and whether this is a territory which is defended.

Most animals which defend territories will fight to repel invaders, but seldom need to do so. Birds use song to mark their boundaries, and this signal is recognised and respected. Mammals may rely on visual signals, or scent. Lemurs, even in a human house, have the unendearing habit of urinating at all their frontier posts, and two lemurs, in one sitting-room, may make two territories and a dreadful smell only to be endured by a lemur-besotted human sharing the premises. The bloodthirsty encounters between moles could occur because they cannot recognise each other before they are locked in mortal combat. Obviously visual signals would be useless, and sounds of only limited range. Scents would seem the most likely means of marking a territory.

The first point which is clear is that, at any rate in such an undisturbed habitat as grass, most moles *do* have well-defined home ranges in which they remain for considerable periods. This has been determined, mainly by trapping experiments and by using radioactive rings, by Gillian Godfrey and J.

Haeck. Fig. 24 gives the sort of picture which may be obtained in grassland at any time of the year, except for males in early spring. Each area was determined in J. Haeck's work by having a grid of 100 Friesian live traps at 10-metre intervals. When first caught, each mole was ringed and the sites of recapture

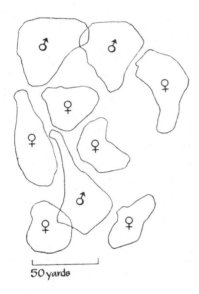

50 yards

FIG. 24 Ranges of moles in pasture.

noted. The traps were moved about at intervals to give better coverage, and to move from sites where the traps had been avoided and new tunnels dug around them. Each range was found to cover about 400 sq. metres and to be of no particular shape. There seemed little difference between the range of males and females. Occasionally there were exceptions, one of which is reported in detail by J. Haeck (see Fig. 25). He found that a female had her range in two parts separated by some 30–40 metres transversed by connecting subterranean pathways. On some days the animal spent part of the time in each section.

At all times slight overlaps in ranges may be observed, but in general, except for spring-time males, the animals in grass-land appear to keep almost completely apart.

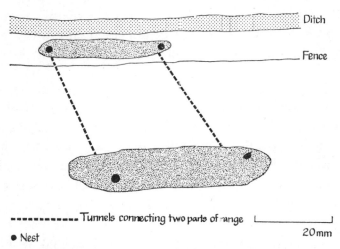

FIG. 25 An unusual range occupied by a mole (after J. Haeck).

The situation just described is not quite static. Some moles may have an almost constant home range for at least several months, most parts of which (which means most sections of the subterranean burrows) are visited daily, but some "drift" does occur. Thus a mole may extend its range in one direction, and contract it in another, gradually over a period of months, with the result that in the end it occupies a new area. Sudden movements over longer distances, particularly by males, do in addition occur.

The most dramatic changes of the range pattern do arise from these male moves in spring. Some may be found to have traversed several burrows of other moles and moved several hundred metres. They do *not* seem to make an instinctive and immediate journey aimed directly towards the nearest female. They may be on the move for several weeks, and certainly continue some time after all the females in the district have become pregnant. At the end of this wandering period they settle down again, perhaps in their original area or something like it.

In woodland there seems to be some more movement. If a mole is caught in a live trap and ringed, it will probably be caught repeatedly at the same site for a week or two, but may then move to another area. Also on several occasions we have caught a different mole in a live trap soon after the original one was caught and put back in the burrow. The overlaps seem greater than in the grassland, but the general pattern seems similar.

So far the picture, then, is of a territorial animal, living in strict isolation, in a rigidly defined territory. Unfortunately the story is much more complicated.

The work so far described does not give any indication of the existence of "main runs," used communally by many moles. It is difficult to see how such a conception fits into the picture. Yet all mole-catchers know they exist, as places where traps can be placed and where catch after catch can be expected. We came across such a site early in our studies in Monks Wood, and the following are the details of our catches:

7. *Above* and *below*, the mole swimming.

8. *Above*, nest and burrows inside a fortress. *Below*, a two-day-old baby mole.

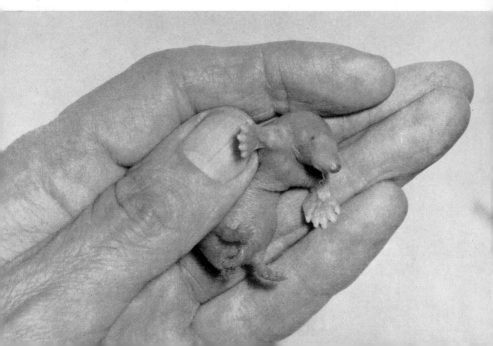

Trap set 6 April

	Examined	Catch
7 April	1000	Male
	1230	Female (pregnant)
8 April	1000	Female (pregnant)
	1530	Male
9 April to 12 April		None caught
13 April	1115	Female (pregnant)

Trap removed

Trap reset 15 July

	Examined	Catch
16 July	1100	Female
	1600	Male
17 July	1215	Male
	1415	Female
18 July	1400	Male

We have had many similar experiences in winter (November) as well as spring and summer. They make nonsense of the story as told so far. The males during April can be accounted for, but why were the females, particularly the pregnant ones, so footloose? Movements in July seem to have been as erratic as those in April. At first I thought that there must be much pressure on the territories and that, as soon as one was vacant, a new occupant moved in. But in April, with the population at its lowest for the year, this seems unlikely. It does suggest that in its original woodland habitat the mole's territorial behaviour was a good deal more fluid than it appears to be in pasture. The main difference between the habitats is, of course, that in the grassland observations, each mole had a discrete tunnel system. In the wood, all the burrows seem to interconnect, and this may affect the behaviour pattern. It would be interesting to see if there were differences in moles from different habitats transferred to grass or woodland. As woodland moles *do* invade surrounding pasture, I expect that no differences would be found.

This explanation, however, does not explain everything, as "main runs" where mole after mole may be caught exist in grassland also. Sometimes mole-catchers have reported predominantly male multiple catches, but, as we have shown, females are often equally numerous.

In arable, the situation is different again. The farmer's activities drive the animals in and out before they have time to parcel out the area neatly as they do in grassland. But the moles still seem to keep themselves to themselves as much as possible.

If, as seems the case at least in grass, moles have territories, how are these defined? A. J. B. Rudge noted that, in his wire tunnels, the moles often excreted near the barriers, and this suggests that territory marking might be by this means (as in lemurs and some other mammals). Others have suggested that moles avoid contact by detecting air currents or other vibrations coming down the tunnels. At present there is no definite information on this subject.

Territorial behaviour has the result of keeping animal numbers below the level where starvation would have this effect. In most habitats moles are much too few to endanger the food supply. Thus in Monks Wood, where we have about two moles to the acre, the biomass of worms, etc. is in the region of a ton. With this magnitude of soil fauna, and allowing each animal an excessive ration of half its own weight of food per day, moles would only need to exhaust some 60 sq. yards of ground in a year. They would, of course, not exhaust it, for many invertebrates would more than keep pace with this rate of consumption. Thus if food were the limiting factor, a mole population of several hundred to the acre would not be impossible. Nowhere has anything of this order of magnitude been observed.

Of course the mole only gets the food entering the burrows, and that found while burrowing. The interesting thing is that the burrows are so often quite widely separated, and much of the space is left unexploited. The strongest argument for territoriality is that the animals do not move up closer together than they do in these rich habitats.

In places like the Breck, the situation is rather different. Food supplies are sparse, and moles cover much larger areas. I think that here food may indeed control densities in a way which does not operate elsewhere. Also we notice that the very poorest peat soils do not appear to be able to support moles. It is not the peat to which they object, for such peat as occurs in East Anglia, where the fauna is richer, has a modest mole population.

In the past we have been unable to study mole dispersal properly, because most suitable habitats are already occupied. We know that after an area is trapped out it is reinvaded quite rapidly, but such work has a limited value. A fascinating opportunity to study dispersal has occurred in the Netherlands, with the creation of the new polder, and the problem here has been

thoroughly investigated by J. Haeck. For full details, his own
report, included in the Bibliography, should be consulted. The
terrain is shown in Fig. 26. The situation is that huge areas of
entirely new land are being created. In 1920, the Afsluitdijk, a
mighty barrier, was closed, cutting off the Zuiderzee from the
North Sea. The lake formed was then named the IJsselmeer.
More than half its area is being turned into new land by
erecting encircling dikes of sand, basalt and boulder clay and
pumping out the water. The level inside is raised by dredging
from the nearby lake bottom. There is a scientifically planned
scheme to turn this somewhat unpromising area into good farmland, growing grass, arable crops and trees, within a remarkably
few years. J. Haeck worked mainly between 1958 and 1964 on
two polders, Nordoost Polder, now almost mature as it had
been drained in 1942, and Oostelijk Flevoland, which had only
been "created" in 1957, though the first dikes were constructed
several years earlier. By the time this work started, the invasion
of the older polder was well advanced, that of the new one just
beginning.

The importance of this work is that it showed that there must
be some factor controlling mole populations, and making the
surplus individuals migrate. In a settled area this cannot be
detected. In Monks Wood, breeding occurs in all the females,
the litters are as big, but the population remains more or less
stable. What happens to the surplus? As we have seen, there is
plenty of food.

The points that seem to me of greatest interest in J. Haeck's
paper are as follows: First, in Oostelijk Flevoland, which is
separated from the mainland by a marginal lake, the Veluwe-
meer, the moles appear to have made their entry by swimming.

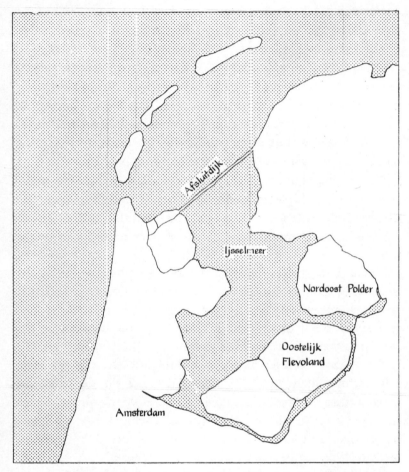

FIG. 26 Map of the areas of reclaimed land in the Netherlands.

This lake is from 200–2,300 metres wide and is only connected by three bridges. The first "molesigns" appeared at various points along the dyke, in places up to more than 600 metres from the mainland, from 1956 onwards. The small islands in the marginal lake were also infested early. Unless we can assume that the mole has some remarkable and unknown sense, to enable it to locate land at such a distance, these moles must represent the fortunate successors of many previous generations which have swum out to sea to be drowned. As we have seen, moles in the fens in Britain swim away from flooded areas, and back when the water recedes. The mainland had not flooded here in Holland, but there is evidently an instinctive reaction to take to the water which must sometimes pay off.

The second finding I think important was that the moles spread and multiplied so quickly. They spread from their foci along the dikes at a rate of 2–3 kilometres (1½–2 miles) a year. The spread was mainly due to the greater mobility of young moles.

Thirdly, the moles followed the food supply, greatest in the dikes and around the fences. I personally was surprised that such a comparatively rich soil fauna, ample for moles, developed so rapidly. As is mentioned in Chapter 5, the moles were the largest and heaviest recorded from any habitat in Europe.

As already mentioned, we do not know what keeps mole populations fairly stable in most areas, nor do we know the usual causes of death, particularly of the older animals which have got established in their burrows. Perhaps they are killed by younger and more vigorous invaders. In the Dutch polders, a higher proportion than usual of all ages must have survived, to cause this quite rapid invasion. Some of the invaders would have drowned had not they found dry land. But drowning cannot be a common cause of death in inland areas and cannot account for much of the normal population control. There was a vole epidemic, and attempts were made to check it by en-couraging kestrels by erecting nest boxes, as there were no trees on the new land and so no natural nesting sites. The small numbers of predators may have been a factor allowing the moles to increase. I think that further analyses of these figures from the Netherlands may give us clues to the factors regulating mole populations in other places.

CHAPTER 10

ECOLOGICAL IMPORTANCE –
THE MOLE AS A PEST

ALL animals have interactions with their environment. In the case of the mole, the most obvious effects are those noticed by farmers and gardeners. Most consider these to be harmful, and so they, and our Ministry of Agriculture, Fisheries and Food, designate the animal as a "pest" or even as "vermin." But the mole has his defenders, who think that, under some circumstances, he does more good than harm. As well as damage – or the reverse – on the farm, the mole has long-term effects on vegetation and the whole economy of other areas, particularly those in which plant growth is rather slow and climatic conditions are extreme.

The enemies of the mole have expressed themselves vigorously for a long time. Thus John Worlidge, in his *Systema Agricultura: The Mystery of Husbandry Discovered*, published as long ago as 1697, says:

> "Moles are a most pernicious Enemy to Husbandry, by loosening the Earth, and destroying the Roots of Corn, Grass, Herbs, Flowers, etc. and also by casting up hills, to the great hinderance of Corn, Pastures, etc."

and Lord Kames, in *The Gentleman Farmer*, in 1776:

> "Molehills may be justly considered as an obstruction to

cropping. It is therefore beneficial to destroy moles; and the simplest way is, to lay hold of the young, which are always found in molehills larger than ordinary."

Coming nearer to to-day, J. P. F. Bell, in *The Agricultural Gazette* in 1904, goes into more detail:

"Owing probably to the comparatively mild nature of recent winters, and to the inattention of occupiers of land, moles have enormously increased in numbers lately, as evidenced by their depredations in all directions. Pasture lands are practically turned upside down, in consequence of which the finer varieties of grasses and clovers suffer severely. When seeds and clover fields are badly infested with moles, great destruction necessarily follows. The soil is disturbed, and the tender rootlets become more susceptible to frost and drought, and a number of the plants die off altogether. Wherever mole hillocks are thrown up the plants are positively up-rooted, and die as a matter of course, whilst on the surface-runs far greater damage is caused than farmers generally are aware of. To a casual observer these are not always easily detected, but they are very apparent to the eye of a naturalist. Whilst moles play sad havoc on pasture land, their dep-redations are infinitely worse on land under tillage. In newly-sown cornfields, especially when laid down with seeds and clover, the damage done by moles is sometimes enormous; and amongst mangel and turnip drills the losses occasioned by these hard-working little animals are almost incalculable. This is especially apparent when farmyard manure is put in the drills; there earthworms are present in abundance and the naturally keen instinct of moles enables them to discover their prey with great facility. Whole acres of plants are frequently destroyed by moles running just under the rootlets and undermining them. Their appetite is insatiable, and they generally hunt for food, and rest, about every three hours alternately, so that half of their existence is spent in a hunt for worms. Many people imagine that moles consume grubs and snails, but there is no authentic record of this having actually been observed, so that worms, if not the absolute, are at any rate the primary food of moles.

"When the economic question of moles versus worms is raised, preference must be given to the latter. Mole hillocks contain no appreciable manurial value, but 'earth-casts' by worms possess a high fertilising power and, in addition to the castings thrown up by worms, which are estimated at many tons per acre during a season, their action produces a process of aeration in the soil which greatly improves its mechanical condition. Professional mole-catchers are fast disappearing, and the art of killing moles is a speciality which untrained men cannot accomplish. This is unfortunate, and may probably be explained by harder times and large areas of land going from tillage to grass. The most favourable time for destroying moles is just before they begin to breed. During their amorous periods their acuteness appears to increase, and they are proportionately difficult to capture. Trapping is more efficacious than poisoning, and by united action on the part of farmers these destructive little animals can very speedily be reduced, much to the benefit of agriculture."

The Ministry's Advisory Leaflet No. 318, 1963 Edition, is more temperate. It simply says:

"The burrowing habit of the mole results in the formation of tunnel-like runs and molehills which, on occasion, are harmful to agriculture. Runs made along the drills of root and grain crops may disturb the roots to such an extent that the crops wilt, or even die. Molehills may cover considerable areas of meadow or cornland and cause damage to the knives of mowing and reaping machines.

"On grazing land, an appreciable area of pasture is sometimes covered by soil thrown up by moles, and this reduces its feeding value. If neglected, molehills may become infested with ants which serve to consolidate and enlarge them. The large grass-covered hillocks often seen on grassland are almost invariably old molehills.

"Moles eat earthworms, and on this account also they are sometimes regarded as harmful. It is doubtful, however, whether the numbers they consume can materially affect the worm population of an area."

Finally, an irate farmer, seeing a newspaper report in which I am quoted as saying they do little damage, writes:

"I find it very sad that a scientist of your calibre and in your position should be responsible for putting out such an untrue statement.

"I am a keen conservationist even to the extent of making gifts of highly strategic areas of land I own or can obtain to Naturalist Trusts, but despair of giving help to people capable of the statements attributed to you.

"On light to medium soil the mole is the greatest pest of grassland we have; it makes the land incapable of being mown; in extreme cases it destroys 20–25 per cent of the crop (I have one such field this year); it makes it impossible to cut and harvest a crop of hay; it prevents the conservation of the grass crop for silage by reason of the admixture of soil in the silo. In all, to have pasture on which you depend on as a reasonable economic unit well stocked with moles is a disaster to the farmer."

However, there is another side to the picture. Edward Jesse, in his *Scenes and occupations of country life: with recollections of natural history*, published in 1853, writes:

"The mole, also, is another of those useful animals which the ignorant and prejudiced of man has doomed to destruction, and against which he wages continual warfare. Such is the impression of the injury done by it that in some parts of Somersetshire the farmers are in the habit of carrying a gun, when they walk in the fields, in case they should see the earth in the act of being turned up by the Moles; when this is the case, the farmer fires at the spot, and thus many Moles are killed in the course of the year.

"So far from the Mole being an injurious, it is a most useful animal to the farmer. It produces hillocks of fine rich mould which are extremely beneficial when spread over the ground – a top dressing of it will invigorate young wheat, whilst the hillocks will suffocate plants, the hills should be scattered more promptly by the farmer. The tunnels keep. the soil drained. The Mole devours the larvae of the cock-chaffer, flies, beetles and wireworm, and when we hear, as we too often do, of the ravages of the wireworm, we may wonder that the very instrument appointed by the Almighty to prevent these ravages should itself be destroyed by man."

Since that date there have been numerous writers who have

praised the mole for devouring pests, and for improving drain-age, while the possible harm caused by removing beneficial earthworms (shown by Charles Darwin in his *Vegetable Mould and Earthworms*, published in 1881) has encouraged a contrary belief. Before 1881 many people thought the earthworms harm-ful and not beneficial to agriculture.

There is, to my mind, no doubt that the mole is a compara-tively minor pest, at least on the national level. Considerable damage can be caused to newly-sown crops by the reinvasion of arable land, and here a vigorous campaign of destruction in the foci of infestation, the ditch banks and hedgerows, during winter, is the best protection. Damage to banks of drainage ditches is also a serious problem, though here the water vole is also a culprit. In the Netherlands there was considerable worry that mole damage would cause re-flooding of the low level polders by causing breaches in the dikes.

Grassland is also damaged. The area covered by the spoil heaps may be considerable, and this obviously reduces the productivity of the area, for bare soil cannot be grazed. The heaps, and the stones in them, may damage the blades of farm machinery. The idea that the hills are a good "top dressing" has little foundation. They may contain subsoil which would *reduce* fertility. The confusion arises from a misunderstanding of Charles Darwin's work on the earthworm. There is no doubt that worm casts – Darwin's "vegetable mould" – is a useful top dressing even if it is disliked by greenkeepers for spoiling the surface of their lawns. But worm casts are, in fact, worm faeces, enriched by admixture with semi-digested vegetable matter. Molehills are unaltered earth. In fact, molehills may, in old grass, interfere with the production of the surface layer of "mould" described by Charles Darwin. An investigation of his sites in 1941 by Sir Arthur Keith and described by P. A. Jewell demonstrates this very clearly. Fig. 27 shows soil profiles in 1841/2, 1871 and 1941. Those in 1841 and 1871 were determined by Charles Darwin. One field, Great Pucklands, had just been ploughed when the observations began. It will be seen that flints are distributed throughout the soil, with many on the surface. It was then put down to grass. By 1871, when Charles Darwin re-examined it, the flints were all buried 3 inches deep in worm casts. By 1941 little change had occurred except that the worms had pulled part of the humus layer below the top flints. In Cricket field, which was grass-covered in 1842, Darwin had scattered chalk lumps on the surface. By 1871 he found them buried 7 inches below wormcasts. The grass obviously contained more surface casting worms than the ploughed field previously mentioned. When the last examination was made in 1941, it was expected that the chalk would be buried even deeper. Instead the confused situation depicted was discovered. Moles had sent some of the chalk to the surface about twenty years previously; this was now buried 3 inches deep. More recent mole activity had sent some chalk again to the surface. This experiment demonstrated the unfortunate effects of mole activity in actually changing the soil surface for the worse.

Mention has already been made of the damage to arable crops by uprooting the plants, and to grass by covering the surface. Another harmful result attributable to moles is known as "pasture reversion." This means that the bare soil from the molehills is colonised by undesirable weeds, mainly non-productive grasses, so that the desirable varieties are eventually reduced, even in the untouched areas. This has been studied on a number of swards. In reseeded upland pastures in Wales

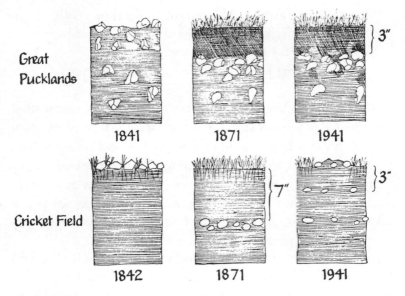

FIG. 27 Effects of worms and moles on the top soil (after C. Darwin, A. Keith and P. Jewell).

it was the best-managed pastures which suffered most. Here the molehills were quickly colonised by *Agrostis tenuis* and other non-productive grasses, sometimes after a succession of other species. The damage to the pasture was often such that re-seeding was necessary. There was no doubt in the farmer's mind that, on his land, the mole was a pest.

Molehills are comparatively easily spread and so may not do much damage to machinery, unless they contain a lot of stones. However, they are often consolidated into much more resistant structures when invaded by ants. This was noted by the poet John Clare who, in a poem quoted *in extenso* in Chapter 11, wrote:

"The pismires (ants, K.M.) too their tip-tops yearly climb
  To lay their eggs and hunt the shepherd's crumbs,
Never disturbed save when for summer thyme
  The trampling sheep upon their dwelling comes."

In Russia, N. P. Voronov noted the same process, but related it to change in the soil and in the vegetation. The anthills, produced from molehills, are much more stable, and resist erosion. They are more exposed to the extremes of summer and winter climate than the general mass of the soil. Meadow grasses are favoured as against woodland species, and this may affect the natural regeneration of woodland as the meadow vegetation can prevent the young trees from growing.

It is difficult to assess the importance of the mole, harmful as a worm-eater, beneficial as a consumer of wireworms and other pests. I do not think it will reduce the worm population significantly in a good soil, but may in a poor one where worms are few but are also badly needed. J. Haeck showed that there was some evidence of a reduction in worms adjacent to mole burrows, but the results were not very great. As to pests, the effect may be considerable, but the mole also eats beneficial species like the Cinnabar Moth, which itself feeds on the troublesome weed, Ragwort. I would hardly think it worth introducing moles to pasture or arable as a form of biological control against insect pests.

The effects of moles in draining the land are also difficult to evaluate. "Moledrains" which are the mechanical equivalent of their efforts are effective, but are placed in the right place and running in the desired direction. The random network made by the living mole can seldom improve drainage; more often it blocks or interrupts existing tile drains. Also moles

9. *Above*, apparatus for keeping live moles. Nest box top left, tunnels made of wire mesh. *Below*, the author examining a Friesian live trap.

10. *Above*, this large molehill was made during the night before the photograph was taken. Note the characteristic appearance of newly-dug soil. This was only one of the hills made by a single mole in one night. *Below*, superficial burrows made by a mole by pushing up the soil surface without needing to make molehills.

seldom work in the waterlogged soils where their efforts might, indeed, be useful.

I think, therefore, that there are few instances when we can prove that moles are beneficial to agriculture, either as pest controllers or as helpers with drainage.

There are several other reported cases of important ecological changes caused by moles. A. S. Watt has, over many years, described the changes in the vegetation at Foxhole Heath in the Breck. He established that the mole played an essential part in the cycle of changes of vegetation observed in several areas. This is described in detail in the paper listed in the Bibliography. In brief, the annual and some of the perennial herbs, which are considered characteristic species of the area, are almost entirely restricted to the bare soil produced by mole activities.

Similarly in Upper Teesdale, A. W. Davison and T. J. Bines found that considerable areas of disrupted turf and bare soil, which persist for several years, are caused by moles. What appears to happen is that the vegetation covered by the new hill dies. In this wet and windy area, the hill blows away, leaving a bare patch of soil which may, over several years, erode down to bare rock. Elsewhere recolonisation is very slow, so the bare patches are longlived.

A final instance of the indirect ecological effects of the mole occurs in the fens. Many trees would not be there but for the efforts of the old mole-catchers. It is fitting to give the last words of this chapter to Arthur Randell, who is here speaking of the use of the traps described on p. 133.

"After a mole stick had been used several times it tended to lose its spring. If my father failed to bend it to make it more pliable, he would take it to the side of a dyke, push it into the wet earth and hang dead moles on it by tying string to their feet. This was to let nearby farmers know that he had been catching on their land. Very often the sticks would take root so that there were, in time, quite a number of willow trees growing in Magdalen Fen which had been 'planted' in this way, and I still know, to-day, where there are three willows and two elders which began as mole sticks."

CHAPTER 11

ENEMIES OF THE MOLE

The Mole-Catcher
by John Clare

When melted snow leaves bare the black-green rings,
  And grass begins in freshening hues to shoot,
When thawing dirt to shoes of ploughmen clings,
  And silk-haired moles get liberty to root,
An ancient man goes plodding round the fields
  Which solitude seems claiming as her own,
Wrapt in greatcoat that from a tempest shields,
  Patched thick with every colour but its own.

With spuds and traps and horsehair string supplied,
  He potters out to seek each fresh-made hill;
Pricking the greensward where they love to hide,
  He sets his treacherous snares, resolved to kill;
And on the willow sticks bent to the grass,
  That such as touched jerk up in bouncing springs,
Soon as the little hermit tries to pass,
  His little carcass on the gibbet hings.

And as a triumph to his matchless skill,
  On some grey willow where a road runs by,
That passers may behold his power to kill,
  On the bough's twigs he'll many a felon tie;

On every common dozens may be met,
　　Dangling on bent twigs bleaching to the sun,
Whose melancholy fates meet no regret,
　　Though dreamless of the snare they could not shun.

On moors and commons and the pasture green,
　　He leaves them undisturbed to root and run,
Enlarging hills that have for ages been
　　Basking in mossy swellings to the sun;
The pismires too their tip-tops yearly climb
　　To lay their eggs and hunt the shepherd's crumbs,
Never disturbed save when for summer thyme
　　The trampling sheep upon their dwelling comes.

This poem indicates that the English countryman was always the greatest enemy of the mole. The mole was considered to be a serious pest. Thus the young girl Anne, in D. H. Lawrence's story, has no doubts: "It's got to be killed, look at the damage they do." Even a humanitarian like Arthur Randell, who clearly has so much respect for his enemy, has the immediate reaction to kill any mole he sees. He recounts an instance of how a friend saw two moles fighting above ground. His immediate reaction was to call to his young grandson: "Kill 'em, boy, you'll never get another chance like this."

Moles have, in the past, been controlled mainly by trapping, a method which continued so long as moleskins had a commercial value. The oldest trap, described in the poem, was used by Arthur Randell's father up to the early years of the present century. It consists (Fig. 28) of two "treacherous snares," with an ingenious system to hold these in place, to release them and to power them so they killed the catch quickly. The trap

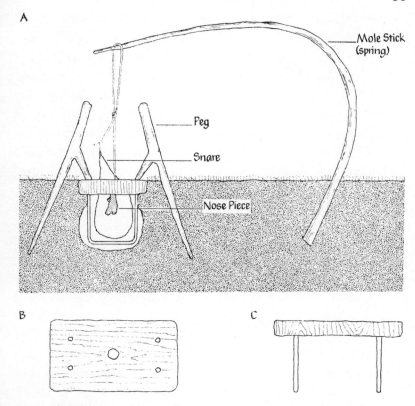

FIG. 28 Home-made mole traps as used in the Fens. A, the trap set, end view; B, board as prepared to make trap; C, side view of board and loops.

consists of a small board with five holes bored through its surface. One, in the middle, marks the situation of the trigger or "nosepiece," a small Y-shaped piece of wood. The snares go through the other holes, and it was usual to have two rigid wooden loops to which the snares were plastered with earth, to enable the snare to be kept open at about the diameter of a mole burrow. This trap had to be kept firmly in position by (usually) three forked pegs. The motive power was a springy stick, often of willow. The trap was set by putting a knot, attached to the stick, through the middle hole and keeping it in position by the nosepiece. The mole was caught when it dislodged the nosepiece. The disadvantage of this trap was that it was difficult and time-consuming to set, and the trapper had to carry a substantial weight of traps, pegs and willow rods.

The first improvement was, instead of the willow rod, the use of an iron spring. This cut out the pegs as well, so the mole-catcher's load was substantially reduced. Two other developments of traps operated by nosepieces were the "whole barrel," which included a wooden tube the diameter of the burrow, and the "half barrel," which substituted a semi-circular wooden gutter, set upside down, for the flat board.

These traps are seldom used to-day. A. J. B. Rudge tried out the "whole barrel" and found that it caught only about a sixth as many moles as the kinds in common use to-day. This may have been partly because the operators were unfamiliar with the mechanism.

The two traps most widely used to-day are the Scissor (Fig. 29) and the Duffus (or metal half barrel) (Fig. 30). The scissor has two strong "jaws" which are held apart by a metal plate. The trap is carefully set on the run, all extraneous soil is removed, and the top is covered over by grass and earth. The mole is caught when it pushes into the trigger plate and displaces it. The animal can be caught approaching from either direction, and it is killed rapidly if not always quite instantaneously.

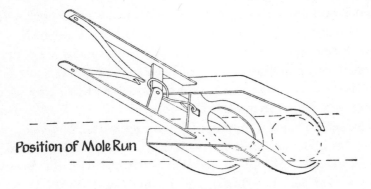

Position of Mole Run

FIG. 29 The Scissor Trap.

The Duffus, which is still a favourite in parts of Scotland, has a metal half barrel and two spring mechanisms essentially similar to a break-back mouse trap. Two moles can, and occasionally are, caught at one trapping.

Both these traps need to be set with care, but trapping is not quite so difficult as some old mole-catchers imply; they are naturally making a mystery of their trade. They often say that new traps must be "weathered" by being left out of doors for some weeks and that great care must be taken in handling the metal. We have found no difficulty in using brand new traps the day they come from the shop. However, Arthur Randell

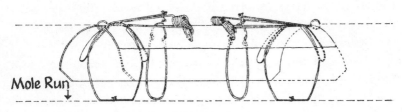

Mole Run

FIG. 30 The Duffus Trap.

reports that when a mole-catcher held a handkerchief saturated with eucalyptus, it appeared to render the traps touched by it ineffective. It may have acted similarly to moth balls (see p. 137), which may be effective mole repellents.

It is actually easy to be disappointed with the results of trapping. Moles frequently dig round and avoid all types, and they set off quite a number by pushing soil and so releasing the catching mechanism. In extensive trials, A. J. B. Rudge only caught moles in 10 per cent of settings with the Scissor, 8 per cent with the Duffus, and 1.5 per cent with the wooden half barrel. I think these results appear worse than they really are, for traps continued to be set for some time after all or almost all the animals in an area had been captured. In areas of woodland, using a dozen strategically placed scissor traps, we have caught moles in the majority at the start of a trapping out period. As mentioned in Chapter 9, some individual trapping sites have yielded catches twice a day for several days. Had the traps been examined more often, even larger numbers might have been killed.

Several other mole traps have been used. The "Harpoon" is deadly. It is set off by a plate which is placed above a burrow which has been trodden down, and when the mole reopens the tunnel, the sharp prongs come down with immense force. Sometimes they may spear a non-vital spot, but they usually cause instant death by squashing as well as piercing. The harpoon trap is difficult to set, and may equally pierce the foot of the operator as the mole he intends to catch.

Fewer and fewer moles are trapped each year; the main method of destruction is poison. The substance most widely used is strychnine, which can only be obtained on the written authority of the divisional offices of the Ministry of Agriculture,

Fisheries and Food. Strychnine may be used against moles, but not against any other pest. It is an extremely poisonous chemical; 5 mg will kill a 500 gm rat. It is unusual for a permit for more than $\frac{1}{4}$ oz (7 gm) to be issued, but this, skilfully used, could kill over 500 moles. The method is to obtain sufficient earthworms, preferably *Lumbricus terrestris*. About ten large worms are needed for an acre. It is as well to avoid the banded, red-brown brandling worm, *Eisenia foetida* (this is often found in manure heaps), as this is not liked by moles. A 1-lb jam jar full of worms can be treated by mixing with $\frac{1}{8}$ oz ($3\frac{1}{2}$ gm) of strychnine. Many mole-catchers prefer to impregnate wool with strychnine, and to thread this along the body of the worm with a darning needle. The worms should be laid, singly, in deep burrows, and the holes must be carefully covered with earth. Obviously great precautions should be taken in using strychnine, to avoid accidents to man, to stock or to wildlife. The ordinary householder is not advised to use this method. If he wishes to get rid of moles, he is advised to use the scissor trap.

Attempts are being made to find a less dangerous poison, but so far nothing seems as good as strychnine. If it is properly distributed, all the moles in an area may be killed within twenty-four hours. Trapping would always be more time-consuming.

Repellents have been used to try to keep a garden free from moles. The method may be considered anti-social as the animals are driven into the neighbours' gardens! Various repellents have been used with varying success. These include moth-balls, sump oil, carbide, smoke bombs (which may, in fact, be lethal). In clay soils quite promising results have been reported, but in light sandy soils high concentrations of smells are not produced, and the animals can easily dig around even the smelliest obstruction.

Another suggestion is to put briars, which may prick the animals' sensitive noses, in the runs. As a rule these are avoided by digging and do not expel the moles.

Certain plants are said to repel moles. The best known is *Euphorbia lathrys*, the Caper Spurge, sometimes called "Mole Spurge." It has been said that, in their second year, Caper Spurge plants will prevent moles coming within 60 yards of where they grow. However, I have had two gardens, on gravel soil in Hertfordshire, and on clay in Huntingdonshire, where moles and Caper Spurge coexist quite happily. I have recently seen one permanent burrow run within inches of a fruiting plant. I am afraid that those who have found that Caper Spurge keeps moles away are mistaken. As the majority of gardens contain no moles anyhow, the plant is being given credit for a condition which would have obtained anyhow!

Gervase Markham, whose extraordinary account printed in 1636 of catching live moles has already been considered (p. 81), also suggested various repellents. These include leeks, garlic and onions, and brimstone burned in a walnut shell. He stated that some of these substances drove the moles on to the surface of the ground, where they fell into a trance and were easily captured. I fear this is also a fictional story.

Man may be the main enemy of the mole, but he is not the only one. Moles are frequently preyed upon by tawny owls, buzzards, herons, ravens and pine martens, and they form an occasional part of the diet of many other predators.

H. N. Southern made a thorough investigation of the diet of the tawny owl, by studying its food pellets. He found that, in summer, almost half the food consisted of moles. During the winter few moles were eaten. It seems that young moles living superficially are the main victims.

J. Haeck has studied the predation of dogs and cats, and has shown that they mainly catch young moles in spring and early summer. Moles killed by motor vehicles while crossing roads were also young and were most frequently killed in summer.

The heron preys on moles in summer to such an extent that one writer suggested that a heron nesting in Regent's Park in London would not succeed because it was likely to be deprived of this item in its diet. Mole remains may appear in more than half the food pellets produced by herons during the summer. A. Hibbert-Ware examined several hundreds of pellets from different localities and found mole fur in 55 per cent. This made the mole the mammal most frequently consumed. Some surprise has been expressed at the ability of the heron to catch moles. I suspect that, in addition to animals on the surface, they can detect movements in superficial burrows and secure their prey with their long beaks.

Moles have shown to be attacked by many parasites, including fleas, ticks and various worms. The so-called mole flea, *Hystrichopsylla talpae talpae*, is our largest flea; it is also found feeding on voles (Fig. 31). It is somewhat surprising to find so many parasites in an essentially solitary animal, and it is difficult to understand how transmission takes place. It has been suggested that many parasites are derived from rodents, weasels, etc. which sometimes use mole burrows.

Work in Czechoslovakia by J. Nosek and I. Grülich showed not only that the virus of Tick-borne Encephalitis (TBE) existed in moles, but also that the carrier of this disease, the tick *Ixodes ricinus*, was found on moles. These workers consider that the mole may be an important reservoir of this disease,

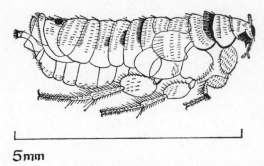

5mm

FIG. 31 The mole flea *Hystrichopsylla talpae*.

which may be transmitted to man. It is probable that the moles picked up the infection by collecting ticks dropped by voles and other animals which entered their burrows. This is the only account I have discovered in which it is suggested that moles may be directly implicated in problems of human health.

CHAPTER 12

OTHER MOLES AND MOLE-LIKE ANIMALS

In Britain we only have one mole, *Talpa europaea*. The same species occurs over much of northern and central Europe, though it may have local races. Whether the giant moles found in the Netherlands (p. 67) are a special race is not known. Various other species have been described, but probably most of these are slight local variations or, at most, local races of *Talpa europaea*. Thus *Talpa romana*, found in Italy, is probably such a race. In southern Europe, including Sicily and Greece, *Talpa caeca* occurs, with a race, sometimes called *Talpa occidentalis*, occupying part of the range. *Talpa caeca* is very like *europaea*, but is said to be completely blind, with a skin flap over its eye, and to be a less vigorous digger, seldom, if ever, making deep burrows. Some workers consider that all European moles are, in fact, the same species.

In Asia we find several races of a closely related mole, *Talpa micrura*. This is depicted in Fig. 32, an old Japanese drawing. It is essentially similar to our own mole, but again it is said to be weaker and not such a successful digger.

The European and Asiatic moles so far mentioned are all true moles, members of the Subfamily Talpinae and the Family Talpidae. They are obviously closely related, so that there is controversy as to their exact division into species. They all live similar lives, differing only, if at all, in their strength and their ability to burrow deeply.

FIG. 32 Old Japanese drawing of a mole, *Talpa micrura*.

In North America there are moles which, while distinct and belonging to other subfamilies (e.g. *Scalopus*), are similar in behaviour and anatomy and are closely related to our European mole. It seems likely that all these animals so far mentioned had a common mole-like ancestor.

The mole belongs to the Order Insectivora, often considered to be the most "primitive" group of placental mammals. This order includes among British mammals the hedgehog and the shrew. In other parts of the world there are several of the Insectivora which do burrow, and show some adaptations to a subterranean life, but none is so specialised as *Talpa*. The Pyrennean Desman or water-mole is its nearest relative, belonging to the same family, the Talpidae. This makes extensive burrows in swampy soil, but its front limbs are comparatively unmodified and it has a long tail. The Golden moles, Chrysochloridae, of South Africa are more mole-like, but they probably represent a separate evolution from an ancestor which did not live underground and was not adapted for digging.

In addition to these insectivorous moles, there have been several quite independent evolutions of burrowing mammals, the end results of which have a remarkable superficial resemblance to *Talpa*, though the animals clearly show in their other characteristics that they belong to widely differing groups of mammals. These "pseudo-moles" have various features in common. They all have bodies which are "mole-shaped." They are blind or nearly so, the external ear is absent or greatly reduced in size, and the tail is short or even vestigial. They all have anatomical modifications to facilitate digging. In some cases this involves the front limbs, as in *Talpa*. In other cases very muscular jaws perform the same function.

The most remarkable case of convergent evolution is the marsupial mole, *Notoryctes typhlops* (Fig. 33). This Australian animal belongs to the Marsupalia and, like the kangaroo, has a pouch in which the young, which are born in a very undeveloped state after a very short gestation period, are suckled and protected until they are able to cope with the outside world. It is remarkably like our own mole in appearance. It is blind, with its eye completely covered over with skin. There is no external ear flap. The front legs are adapted for digging, though the details of the skeletal and muscular structures, and of the hands, are quite different from *Talpa*. The marsupial mole lives in dry, sandy soil, where it constructs its burrows. Little is known about its habits and mode of life in the wild. In captivity it is carnivorous, and will eat "a handful of worms" in a few

FIG. 33 Marsupial mole *Notoryctes typhlops*.

minutes. It drinks water or milk readily. It is described as very restless, as is *Talpa*, but may differ in having longer periods of rest when its rate of metabolism falls. This could enable it to survive in its unpromising habitat. It is as difficult to understand how the marsupial mole obtains sufficient food in the dry and rather unproductive soil in which it occurs, as it is to understand how our own mole survives in the not so dissimilar dry areas of the Suffolk Breck. *Notoryctes* has never been found in the moister and more productive areas of Australia. One interesting similarity with *Talpa* is that, during activity, *Notoryctes* carries its short, stumpy tail erect.

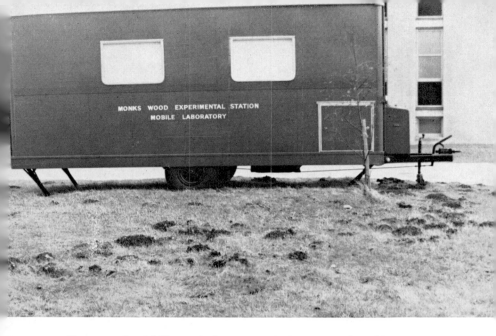

11. *Above*, patch of hills made by one mole in one week. This area had no moles or burrows before this invasion by a single mole. *Below*, molehills on Parsonage Down in Wiltshire. This area of old grassland on thin soil over chalk has a fairly sparse invertebrate fauna, so many molehills are made by few moles making an extensive burrow system to collect food.

12. *Above*, mole tracks in the snow. *Below*, molehill forced up through the snow.

Among the rodents, the order containing such animals as rats and mice, there are several mole-like species. The mole-rat *Spalax* (Fig. 34) is found in eastern Europe. It is a mole-shaped rodent, about $1\frac{1}{2}$ to 2 times the size of *Talpa*. It is blind as the tiny eyes are covered by an opaque cornea, it has no external ear, and only a vestigial tail. The limbs are quite "rat-like" and not specially modified for digging. The animal digs quite differently from *Talpa*, mainly using its powerful incisor teeth,

FIG. 34 Mole rat, *Spalax hungaricus*.

and the massive head with its muscular jaw is the main anatomical feature related to its mode of life. This mode of life is, superficially, very like that of our mole. Each animal has its own separate tunnel system, and this may be recognised by the presence of heaps of soil which look like molehills. Some of these, like the fortresses of *Talpa*, contain nests. Except during the breeding season the sexes are as antagonistic to each other as in *Talpa*. The main difference from *Talpa* is that *Spalax* is a vegetarian, and it has to keep extending its burrows to feed on plant roots, bulbs and corms. In cultivated areas it may be a pest, eating potatoes, carrots and root crops. Some green food is collected above ground. *Spalax* stores its vegetable foods in the same way that *Talpa* may store earthworms.

In South Africa we find the Free State mole, *Cryptomys*. Its general behaviour is similar to *Spalax*. It makes a complex burrow system, leading from its nest to the areas of extension which are the feeding grounds. Experiments have shown that *Cryptomys* is possibly even more skilful than *Talpa* in avoiding broken runs and burrowing accurately for distances of many feet to find the other end of the undamaged tunnel. Digging is done mainly with the teeth. *Cryptomys* is much larger than most mole-like animals, reaching a weight of 6 lbs (2.7 kg). It is said to be good to eat. Unlike most of the moles and pseudo-moles, *Cryptomys* is considered to be beneficial to soil and to pasture. Its food consists mainly of harmful plants, particularly bulbs of the "wild tulip" *Homeria* and the nut grass *Cyperus esculentus*, and it does undoubtedly reduce their numbers and allow more desirable plants to invade the areas containing the burrows. Regarding its general ecology, G. Elloff of the University of the Orange Free State writes: "Various observations have been made, and all have convinced us of the great importance of molehill openings in letting water, during heavy rains, run into the soil in a manner very similar to that done by the cracks in turf soil. There is also no doubt that the molehills alone, without the exposure of the lateral tunnels by the wind, have a most beneficial effect on the soil, for not only is the soil turned up, but the resultant increased porosity ensures the admission of water and air." He also showed that *Cryptomys* tends to prevent serious soil erosion.

These are only some of the cases of convergent evolution, showing how the mole's anatomic features, developed in other animals in different ways, are suited to its mode of life. Many other animals make burrows, without needing special anatomical adaptations. In most cases, e.g. the rabbit, the anatomy is adapted to the more vulnerable time spent above and not below the earth. It presumably does not matter that their sporadic digging is not very efficient.

Mammals are not the only creatures which are adapted to dig. Some reptiles live underground, but show few adaptations. Earthworms are, of course, burrowers *par excellence*, but they have adopted a quite different technique from the mole and the pseudo-moles. However, a remarkable similarity is found among the Insecta, where the most amazing mole-like adap-

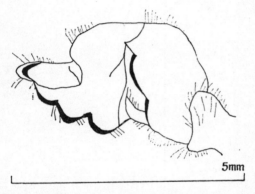

5mm

FIG. 35 Front leg of mole cricket, *Gryllotalpa*.

tation is found in the mole cricket *Gryllotalpa*. This insect has its front legs adapted most efficiently for digging (Fig. 35) and they do resemble superficially the front legs of *Talpa*. The insect lives in a burrow in damp soil and has become less common in recent years in Britain, being now apparently restricted to localities around the New Forest. At one time *Gryllotalpa* was looked upon as a pest, and has even invaded glasshouses and damaged tomatoes. We have only one species, *Gryllotalpa gryllotalpa*, though there are other species in other countries.

Although they can and do dig most efficiently, their burrow is protective and, possibly, acts as a resonator to amplify the noise made by the male to attract a female. They feed mainly outside on living plants. Nevertheless, their bizarre resemblance to *Talpa* makes them a suitable subject with which to conclude.

BIBLIOGRAPHY

THERE is an immense literature about moles. I only include here a limited number of the older scientific papers as very full bibliographies are given by Godfrey and Crowcroft (1960) and by Haeck (1969). In many cases I give brief notes after the particulars of a book or paper. These are not intended as summaries, but to indicate something of the content of the book or paper and of the level of specialisation intended by the author.

Ardrey, Robert (1967). *The Territorial Imperative*. Collins, London. [Also (1969) in Fontana paperback.] Stimulating reading by a first-rate popular writer, sometimes infuriating to scientists.

Barrett-Hamilton, G. E. H. and Hinton, M. A. C. (1910–21). *A History of British Mammals*. Gurney and Jackson, London. Discursive and readable, still the best source for much older material on some mammals.

Burt, W. H. (1943). Territoriality and home range concepts as applied to mammals. *J. Mammal.* 24: 346–352. An important paper introducing these topics to research workers.

Deanesly, R. (1966). Observations on reproduction in the mole, *Talpa europaea*. *Symp. zool. Soc. Lond.*, No. 15, 387–402. Seasonal changes in reproductive organs.

Dubost, G. (1968). Les mammifères souterrains. *Rev. Ecol. Soc. Sol.*, 5: 99–133. Comparative account of mammals (Marsupials, Insectivors, Rodents) which live underground. (In French.)

Eloff, G. (1954). The Free State Mole (*Cryptomys*). *Farming in South Africa*, June 1954. Popular account of beneficial effects of mole activity.

Evans, A. C. (1948). The identity of earthworms stored by moles. *Proc. zool. Soc. Lond.*, 118: 356–359. Showed they were mostly *Lumbricus terrestris* with their heads bitten off.

Gerard, B. M. (1964). Lumbricidae (Annelida). *Linnean Soc. Lond.*, *Synopses of British Fauna* No. 6. Describes all British earthworms, with keys to identify species.

Godfrey, G. and Crowcroft, P. (1960). *The Life of the Mole* (*Talpa europaea* Linnaeus). Museum Press, London. Out of print but can be borrowed from many libraries. A useful summary, with a full account of Gillian Godfrey's own excellent work. Extensive bibliography, which includes other papers by Gillian Godfrey.

Grülich, I. (1967). Zur Methodik der Alterbestimmung des Maulwurfs, *Talpa europaea* L., in der Periode seiner selbständigen Lebensweise. *Zool. Listy* 16: 41–59. Method of telling the age of moles by the amount of wear of their teeth.

Haeck, J. (1969). Colonisation of the mole (*Talpa europaea* L.) in the IJsselmeer polders. *Netherlands Journal of Zoology* 19: 145–248. Account by a research worker, not easy reading for the amateur. Excellent bibliography.

Hope Jones, P. (1969). Distribution of moles in part of Merioneth. *Nature in Wales* 11: 164–168.

Jewell, P. A. (1958). Natural History and Experiment in Archaeology. *Advmt Sci.* 15: 165–172. An examination of the fields where Charles Darwin studied the production of stone-free topsoil ("vegetable mould") by earthworms, and how moles have upset the stratification of the soil.

Matthews, L. Harrison (1935). The oestrous cycle and inter-sexuality in the female mole (*Talpa europaea* Linn.). Proc. *Zool. Soc. Lond.* 1935: 347–382. Scientific investigation explaining the countryman's belief that, except during the breeding season, "all moles are males."

Matthews, L. Harrison (1968). *British Mammals.* Collins, London. Authoritative and comprehensive but comprehensible to the general reader.

Mellanby, K. (1967). Food and activity in the mole, *Talpa europaea. Nature, Lond.* 215: 1128–1130. Experiments on captive moles, on periodicity of activity and food consumption.

Milner, C. and Ball, D. F. (1970). Factors affecting the distribution of the mole (*Talpa europaea*) in Snowdonia (North Wales). *J. Zool., Lond.* 162: 61–69. Moles and soil types at high altitudes.

Ministry of Agriculture, Fisheries and Food (1963). *The Mole.* Advisory Leaflet 318. H.M. Stationery Office. Short, accurate with information about control.

Oppermann, J. (1968). Die Nahrung des Maulwurfs (*Talpa europaea* L. 1758) in unterscheidlichen Lebensraumen. *Pedobiologia* 8: 59–79. Research paper. Detailed investigation of mole food in meadow, woodland, etc.

Quilliam, T. A. (Convener and Editor) (1966). The mole: its adaptation to an underground environment. Proceedings of a Ciba Guest Meeting, 5 and 6 January 1966. *J. Zool. Soc. Lond.* 149: 31–114. A series of research papers by different workers. They include:

Mellanby, K. Mole activity in woodlands, fens and other habitats, 35–41.

Rudge, A. J. B. Catching and keeping live moles, 42–45.

Morris, Patrick. The mole as a surface dweller, 46–49.

Raw, F. The soil fauna as a food source for moles, 50–54.

Yalden, D. W. The anatomy of mole locomotion, 55–64.

Earl of Cranbrook. Notes on the relationship between the burrowing capacity, size and shoulder anatomy of some eastern Asiatic moles, 65–70.

Holmes, R. L. The pituitary gland of the mole in relation to that of other insectivores, 71–75.

Quilliam, T. A. The mole's sensory apparatus, 76–88.

Graziadei, P. Electron microscopic observations of the olfactory mucosa of the mole, 89–93.

Lund, R. D. and Lund, Jennifer S. The central visual pathways and their functional significance in the mole (*Talpa europaea*), 94–101.

Crawford, B. H. Perception underground: Review of physical aspects and measurements, 102–106.

Morris, P. Mole footprints and heaps, 107–108.

Rudge, A. J. B. Techniques and apparatus used in mole research, 108–109.

Armsby, A., Quilliam, T. A. and Soehnle, H. Some observations on the ecology of the mole, 110–111.

Aldrich, A. and Quilliam, T. A. Some aspects of mole behaviour, 112–113.

Randell, Arthur (1970.). *Fenland Mole-catcher*. Routledge and Kegan Paul. Genuine account of a countryman's experiences.

Raw, F. (1959). Estimating earthworm populations by using formalin. *Nature, Lond.* 184: 1661–1662. A method for studying worm populations. Also useful in producing many large *Lumbricus terrestris* to feed moles. Such should be quickly washed in water and kept in soil until needed.

Skoczen, S. (1958). Tunnel-digging by the mole (*Talpa europaea* Linne.). *Acta Theriologica, Biclowieza* 2: 235–249. In English. The most important paper on this subject on the European mole.

Watt, A. S. (1947). Pattern and process in the plant community. *J. Ecol.* 35: 1–22.

Watt, A. S. (1971). Factors controlling the floristic composition of some plant communities in Breckland. In *Scientific Management of Animal and Plant Communities for Conservation*, edited by E. Duffey and A. S. Watt. British Ecological Society Symposium, Volume No. 11. Vegetation patterns now shown to be largely caused by mole activity.

INDEX